The X Y Z of Love

Inge and Sten Hegeler

The X Y Z of Love

Frank answers to every important question
about sex in today's world

With drawings by Eiler Krag

Translated from the Danish by David Hohnen

MacGibbon & Kee London

Granada Publishing Limited
First published in Great Britain 1970 by MacGibbon & Kee Ltd
3 Upper James Street, London W1R 4BP
Reprinted 1970, 1971 (twice)

Copyright © 1968 by Inge and Sten Hegeler
This translation copyright © MacGibbon & Kee Ltd 1970. The
original is slightly abridged
First published under the title *Spørg Inge & Sten* by Rhodos,
Copenhagen, 1968

ISBN 0 261 63207 8
Printed in Great Britain by Compton Printing Ltd
London and Aylesbury

Contents

Foreword

This book has been compiled from various sources. To start with, we have taken some of the best questions from *Femina*, a Danish women's weekly. We have also taken a good many from our correspondence column in *Ekstrabladet*, a Danish midday paper.

In addition, however, a number of questions and answers have been selected from the letters we have received during the past twenty years—these amount to some fifteen thousand.

Nobody who has confided anything to us in writing need feel nervous. Nobody's identity will be revealed.

We have permitted ourselves to go a little further in this book —and a little deeper—than is possible in the columns of a daily newspaper. For pedagogical reasons it has been impossible to avoid a certain amount of repetition. On the other hand, questions have not been divided up proportionately. This has enabled us to touch on one or two matters of a more specialized nature.

Our chapter headings should not be taken too literally. Readers will often be able to find an answer in a completely different chapter from the one they might have picked on at first sight.

This book has not been written for very young people, who wouldn't be able to understand things that can be problems for older people. Nevertheless, we felt it would be a good thing to include a small selection of questions from the younger age groups.

We very much enjoy hearing from readers. This book really only amounts to what one might call a pause in transit. We shall continue to give advice and information in our correspondence column.

Readers are welcome to send us questions, criticism, corrections and supplementary information. Sexual enlightenment is still a relatively neglected field.

Inge and Sten Hegeler

PS: It is difficult to phrase the right kind of warning, but we feel we must advise delicate souls, or readers who are easily shocked, to refrain from reading this book. We say this not with the object of whetting anybody's appetite, but merely because we don't want to hurt or offend anybody.

And another thing: we can't (and don't) expect everybody to share our sense of humour.

1. Happiness is . . .

In this chapter we outline the thoughts and ideas underlying our way of running a correspondence column. They are taken from an interview which appeared in connection with the correspondence column which we started in a Danish newspaper.

Q: *So you're going to start a correspondence column on SEX, are you?*

A: *We* don't feel it need be restricted exclusively to sex, but of course there are bound to be a good many questions on the subject. After all, it's an important and often very problematical part of everyday life. It's up to our readers to decide what it's to become.

Q: *Are there any questions you can't answer?*

A: A lot. We don't claim to know everything. In some cases we have to ask others before we can answer. And there's a special category we can't cope with, and that's the purely medical question.

Q: *Do you stick to any sort of rule in formulating your answers?*

A: Yes! We feel no question is too minor or unimportant to be answered. We've formed the impression that readers intend their questions seriously, that the question means a great deal to the questioner. So no matter what the question is, we feel we have no right to dismiss it with a witty or impertinent answer.

Q: *What about anonymous questions?*

A: We don't mind if readers ask us things without telling us
their names and addresses. We know some people prefer to
keep their names a secret. They're fully entitled to if they
write to us.

Q: *But presumably you're bound to professional secrecy?*

A: Of course! Nobody else apart from the two of us opens the
letters we receive, or reads them. As soon as we've copied
out the contents we burn them.

Q: *Quite honestly, Inge Hegeler, do you believe correspondence
column answers can help anybody? Can a marriage that's on
the point of busting up be saved just by writing to you?*

A: Obviously, to try to give advice in a correspondence column
is very difficult. We don't get all the details. We hear only
one side. Nevertheless, it's our experience that correspondence columns have a mission. We may be lucky enough to
throw some light on some aspects which the questioner
hadn't thought of. In many cases the person asking the
question thinks that he or she is abnormal—or that his/her
partner is. If so, we can sometimes help by saying a few
things about what we're all like, basically. We may be able
to help some people to face up to themselves, and to the
other person—to learn to *accept* a little more.

Q: *Inge and Sten Hegeler, is your correspondence column going
to be the best in the world, or have you a hero, a model, to
look up to?*

A: We're great fans of Harry Jensen's correspondence column
on motoring matters in *Motor*, the magazine published by
the Danish Association of Automobile Owners. We hope
our readers—just like his—will be able to take a good story
once in a while. There's no reason why it should make us

lose our sense of objectivity or respect for those who pose us questions.

We're very taken with a question in *Motor* from a motorist who says that even though he creeps into his bedroom late at night as quietly as he can, his wife always kicks up a tremendous fuss. 'Can you suggest any way of getting rid of this sort of engine trouble?' he asks Harry Jensen, who immediately replies: 'Well, you're going about it quite the wrong way! You should roar into the garage, slam the door, and tramp up the stairs singing "Your tiny hand is frozen" at the top of your voice. Then, as you crawl into bed, you should give your wife a hearty slap on the highest point of her eiderdown and say: "Well, Daisy," (or whatever her name is), "how's about it, old girl?" Then I can *guarantee* you she'll pretend to be asleep—very sound asleep.'

Q: *Can you tell a similar story?*

A: Do you know the one about the Turk who wanted to send his old mother a picture of himself? Unfortunately the only snapshot he could find was one in the nude, but he decided he could just cut it in two and send the top half. But as luck would have it he put the *bottom* half in the envelope by mistake. At Easter he got a postcard from his mother, who wrote: 'My dear boy—Thank you for your letter. You're getting more and more like your father. You've grown a beard and your tie seems to be hanging a bit crooked.'

Q: *In connection with what sort of question would you feel like using that story?*

A: It could probably be used in connection with a question about modern art. I think the man's old mother in Turkey showed she had an open mind—which is more than one can say for many opponents of modern art.

Q: *Is there nothing you take seriously?*

A: The expression 'to take things seriously' somehow has an echo of traditions, taboos and misplaced respect. We're disrespectful in our way, but we try to answer sincerely. We also believe in humour as an antidote against those who take themselves too seriously.

Q: *Do you want to help people to be happier?*

A: By all means, if we can!

Q: *Big words!*

A: Possibly. But we still don't think we overestimate the value of a correspondence column.

Q: *Does it make people any happier to read about other people's unhappiness, other people's problems?*

A: A correspondence column isn't only helpful to the person who writes and asks about something. It can be just as helpful to the many other people who happen to have the same or similar problems.

Q: *Do you know the meaning of happiness?*

A: We know what it means to be happy—each of us individually, and especially together. But of course there are always problems. A life completely without problems wouldn't be worth living.

    But the problems shouldn't be too big. Problems shouldn't be insuperable. You should always have a feeling of being capable of dealing with them—that you're just about to solve them.

Q: *Yes, but what is happiness?*

A: We've seen many definitions of happiness. None of them

covers everything. We have a definition too—and ours is also only partly true, but we might use it as a part of our motto for our correspondence column:

Happiness is knowing what is normal, knowing what other people do.

And 'normal' covers a wide range.

2. Our readers speak their minds

This chapter provides space for criticism, irritation and correction from our readers. This is important.

Only One Factor

We enjoy reading your many good answers to people with problems, but we're surprised you never seem to touch on the most important thing about living together with another person, namely love.

Enjoying the interplay of little things,
Feeling like doing what the other person wants to do,
Quietly saying the big things,
Sharing bed and board . . .

All this talk about orgasms and so on is quite in order and important, but it's still only one of the factors that go to make up two people's life together.

We don't disagree with you, nor with the author of the lines you quote, the late Poul Henningsen, Denmark's tireless and utterly uncompromising champion of liberalism and plain thinking (and our acknowledged hero and ideal).

But on the other hand our contributions to this column are governed by two things. First, what we ourselves believe we know a little about. And even though we can be both loving and romantic together in private (thank heavens!) we feel we know more about SEX than LOVE.

Secondly, it's the questions we get from our readers that decide the issue.

Perhaps we could illustrate what we mean by mentioning that we never get letters saying: 'We get on marvellously in bed, but love is our big problem.'

But we get masses of letters that say: 'We love each other deeply, but I never get sexual satisfaction, never have an orgasm.'

This is where most of the problems seem to lie. Thanks for your letter.

i. & s.h.

Tired of Liberal Outlook

I'm tired of your idiotically liberal outlook! We'd only just got rid of you in a weekly magazine, and now you turn up here.

May I ask you a straight question? Do you really go in for this wave of seedy pornography that's swamping us all at present, and has been doing so for so many years? After all, it's downright harmful.

In the old days, bad authors wrote bad pornography. Now we've reached the point where good authors write bad pornography. This is only a transitional phase. Now that the law in Denmark has been made less strict, there's a chance of good authors starting to write good pornography.

This is the shortest way we can answer you. Let us add that we're proud to live in a country where the law is so lenient—and that we hope it will become even more so.

You might ask us what we understand by pornography. Answer: descriptions of the entire sexual side of people's lives. Good pornography is an honest, truthful description, whereas bad pornography is false, hypocritical and twisted.

And now for the point about being 'downright harmful'. We believe, in principle, that suppression does more harm than frankness.

Finally, we'll fully admit that most of the pornography that has appeared in recent years is misleading as it has been written by men and is thus more a reflection of their daydreams than of reality; or by women who've fallen for men's daydreams and believe that's the way girls are.

But if we start applying censorship, we'll never agree. The same applies to art in general. Take a couple of Hans Andersen's fairy-tales like *Little Claus and Big Claus* and *The Tinderbox*, both of which are such glorifications of psychopathic behaviour, of utterly egoistic lack of consideration, that they'd be forbidden if we censored children's books—and didn't know Hans Andersen had written them. Try reading the two tales again some time!

But if we let the chaff past at least we get the wheat as well.

i. & s.h.

Shame on You!

Do you realize you're responsible for the fact that so many young girls mess up their lives nowadays and produce one illegitimate bastard after another?

It's you who encourage young people to behave wantonly. It wasn't like that sixty years ago when my husband and I were young!

Sixty years ago more children were born out of wedlock per one thousand inhabitants in Denmark than today.

i. & s.h.

They're Laughing at You

You're so damned broad-minded and understanding it makes one sick. You also invite people to write to you anonymously if they want to.

Tell me, has it never dawned on you that many of the people who write to you anonymously are just taking the mickey out of you? Has it really never occurred to you?

Once in a while we suspect something of the sort, but does it matter?

i. & s.h.

Sex-Jabber

Is this country really sick, or is it me? Because all this jabber about SEX is enough to make one puke. Why do you churn out all this filth, thereby making the streets unsafe for all our sweet young girls?

Think of all the girls who get attacked and raped on account of what you're doing—and on account of all these filthy pornographic books you find everywhere. And films.

I know girls who've got other thoughts in their heads—and I have fun with them.

Remember, chaps, that girls can be used for better things!

To put it briefly: a girl's friendship is worth more than gold.

You seem to be well up in what is happening in the porno-graphic field, but you overlook the fact that the so-called Pornographic Wave has not led to an increase in the number of sexual crimes—on the contrary.

'There's such a lot of talk about sex today,' so you claim, and many others, but it's not true. There's always been a lot of talk about sex and everything connected with it—except during a brief, prudish interlude. And a lot has been written about it too.

Many thousands of erotic books have been written before you and we were born, so it's not a 'new' fashion at all. By the way, do you realize that sexual crimes in this country have dropped about 25 per cent? Actually *diminished*?

So we can prove that neither books, films nor our own activities (to which you are kind enough to draw attention) have caused any increase in rape.

If there should be any sort of connection, on the one hand, between the present-day free-and-easy way of talking about sex, and on the other, sexual crimes—well, it can only be a favourable one.

i. & s.h.

We're Fine!

So happiness is supposed to be knowing what is normal! But all these people who have to get themselves rubberwear, governesses, garlic and lord knows what—do you mean to tell me they're not abnormal?

How about cleaning up our minds instead, and getting some of those noble feelings going again? Isn't it more than enough if two people love each other and gaze deeply into each other's eyes? Or are we abnormal because we manage without all these monkey tricks?

After twenty-seven years together, we've still got our love to keep us warm, and we have lovely memories going right back to the days when we were young.

We've had sadness and upsets in between too—and a bit of unfaithfulness as well, but we just think of the good side.

Our advice to those who can't get on is: 'Think of something else! Just think about each other, about making each other happy, and then things'll work out by themselves.'

If you're getting on so nicely and have so few problems, isn't it a bit intolerant of you to reject the possibility that others may be having a more difficult time of it?

Isn't it a little facile and naïve to tell those who happen to be less fortunate than yourselves merely to clean up their minds and gaze deeply into each other's eyes?

It would be nice if *you* were right.

i. & s.h.

Corny Jokes

I'm prepared to accept people who attempt to give the younger generation objective and serious information about sex.

But I feel you drag man's nobler, finer feelings down in the mire with your silly, corny jokes.

Of course our jokes are old. We don't make them up ourselves, so somebody's always heard them before.

If man's nobler, finer feelings can't stand up to a good old
laugh once in a while we haven't much time for them. And we
believe that humour, or a joke, is a good way of getting things
on to a more understandable, everyday level.

We have a soft spot for Svend Johansen, the Danish painter,
and very nearly agree with him when he says: 'It doesn't matter
if a joke is dirty provided it's coarse.'

There's a deeper meaning below the surface of that statement.

i. & s.h.

Invented Letters

*Tell me quite honestly, don't you write all these questions and
answers yourself? If I'm right—that you make them up yourself—
then I don't suppose you'll answer me truthfully. But the questions
seem so well written. I'm not saying your correspondence column
isn't fun to read anyway.*

You don't leave us much chance of being believed. You
declare beforehand that we'll probably lie to you.

It may be difficult to convince you, but we can tell you that
we get so many questions every week we could easily fill up the
whole paper with them every Monday—and then some.

Now there *are* a number of questions that keep on turning up,
and so we don't need to answer each one individually. We
answer many letters privately. But at all events it's quite
unnecessary for us to spend our time *inventing* questions.

We shorten the questions we get quite a bit. Sometimes we
may change the age and number of children and other clues that
might make the questioner recognizable. And finally we correct
spelling mistakes and that sort of thing—which, we admit, takes
away some of the original, genuine flavour of the letter. And
perhaps this is what has struck you as being a bit false. You're
right here *up to a point*—but we feel it would be giving people

away a shade too much if we printed all letters in their original form.

i. & s.h.

PS. Even our best friends and acquaintances ask us now and then: 'You write the questions yourselves, don't you?'

We don't quite know what to do to get rid of this suspicion. We have a constant pile of between two hundred and four hundred letters lying unopened—weighing heavily on our consciences. People waiting for answers! In other words, an enormous selection, which means we certainly don't need to think up questions ourselves.

Listen Here!

As you seem to have the idea that a woman's clitoris is the decisive factor contributing to her sexual satisfaction, I feel I must refer you to the psychoanalyst Jo Jacobsen's book Sexual Reform. *On page 69 she writes: 'A little girl, when she reaches the age of puberty, has to advance to the normal form of vaginal eroticism, and if this is to take place the path, during the genital period, must lead, first through penis-envy and thereafter through the father, to the wish for a child. It is only after this that contact with the mother can be established in the right way, i.e. through sublimation. Here it is important not to let the child become bound too strongly to the father, or be harmfully rejected . . . etc.'*

Thank you for your letter, which gives us an opportunity to amplify our views.

May we answer you with a parable?

Once upon a time there was a man who claimed that a proper sneeze came from somewhere up in the palate. Grown-up, mature people sneezed up in the roofs of their mouths and not through their noses. Sneezing through the nose was childish nonsense. And everybody shamefully concealed the fact that they sneezed through their noses and went to a lot of trouble trying to sneeze through their mouths instead.

We might cite Hans Andersen's story *The Emperor's New Clothes* too.

Do you understand what we mean?

The superstition about vaginal orgasm is plain *foolishness*. We express ourselves strongly because generations of women have suffered from having been stamped as abnormal and childish.

The fact that a lady might have sneezed through her mouth in Southern Siberia in 1869 leaves us utterly cold! The important thing to us is that healthy, normal, happy women with good sex lives, mature and experienced women, i.e. the overwhelming majority of women who get something out of their sexual relations with their husbands—all these women stress the great importance of the clitoris as the organ that 'switches on the orgasm'. The vagina is utterly unimportant in this connection *compared with the clitoris*.

'Vaginal orgasm' is a persistent myth that merely serves to delay a woman's sexual development. No scientist has been able to find the nerve centres in the vagina that are supposed to be so important—on the contrary. The vagina is comparatively insensitive.

i. & s.h.

PS. This is not saying that a woman has no feelings in her vagina. But the feelings pass via the clitoris. Once a woman has made sure of her orgasm she can start enjoying the more distant sensations—in her vagina, for instance.*

Boring Barrel-Organ

I've been reading your correspondence column ever since it started, and used to think you were fun, on the ball and useful.

Your column has also gradually become bolder and more outspoken. I dare say it's about the most frank column of its kind in existence. I'm trying to be fair to you.

But seriously, aren't you beginning to get a little bit boring? Aren't you repeating yourselves rather a lot? Couldn't you find some way of—well, putting a new tune in your old barrel-organ?

We're sure you're perfectly right. We certainly do get a lot of letters with the same problems, and it would be a bit silly if we started giving different answers.

We're aware of the problem. Faithful readers in particular must be getting heartily tired of us and the way we campaign for the same things over and over again. But new readers come along

---

* Controversy over the causes and nature of clitoral as distinct from vaginal orgasm has lasted for fifty years. Freud's (unscientifically based) theory of a change from a clitoris-based libido in childhood to a vagina-based libido in womanhood led to the commonly held view of clitoral orgasm as indicating immaturity, neuroticism and masculinity, and vaginal orgasm maturity, normality and femininity. This view has come under increasing criticism in the last twenty years. Kinsey (1953), Albert Ellis (1953), Masters and Johnson (1960–2) and others propounded the primacy of the clitoris in orgasm. At the same time, the gynaecologist Kegel concluded (1953) that the physiological basis of vaginal orgasm involves certain nerve endings in the vaginal walls that may be stimulated by the penis, and found that strengthening of these muscles by exercise can enhance sexual response in the vagina. Within the last few years Masters and Johnson have effectively ended the controversy by proving that the same orgasmic responses can occur after clitoral *or* vaginal stimulation (and sometimes stimulation of the breasts alone), and that the clitoris is stimulated (by the penis or male pubic area) simultaneously with the vagina during ordinary coitus.—*Ed.*

now and then, people who may not have heard what we have to say.

Others need to read things several times before they really sink in—not because they are foolish, dense or slow in the uptake, but because some of the things we say are very novel to the persons in question, and often in marked opposition to accepted attitudes that have come down over the generations.

We believe then that you're quite right, and that we can't help boring a number of readers. Sexual relations *are* really rather boring—to read about, to watch on film, etc. It's much more fun when you're in the thick of things yourself, trying to solve the problems.

Unfortunately we can't promise to change our ways very much. The problems, after all, are very much the same from one little home to the next.

Incidentally, our correspondence column has always been open to other questions besides those about sexual problems, but 99·9 per cent of the letters we get *are* concerned with sex.

Thanks for the criticism.

i. & s.h.

3. Women about men—and about themselves

In this chapter, women write mainly about their problems with men: energetic men, imaginative men, boring men and men who just can't be bothered. The saddest thing for all parties is to see the sexual silence in which so many people live together. They can't talk about matters concerning their own personal relations with one another. Things could have been so good, but instead they fail to make contact.

All too many couples have turned into two singles.

My Unfaithful Husband

I've just discovered that my husband has been unfaithful to me— not with anybody that meant anything to him, just 'for the fun of it'.

I got so furious it very nearly caused our marriage to break up, but now I'm trying to forgive him. It's not easy.

How do I restore the balance in our little home?

I thought of going out and being unfaithful to him in return. Do you think it would be the answer?

It sounds as though it could be an answer, but we don't think so—for several reasons.

It would be better to get yourself a new hat or a new dress that could make you look prettier.

We believe the balance should be restored, but not by means of revenge and retribution. Men have organized things very cunningly. A man's unfaithfulness turns him into a hell of a fellow whom you really ought to be thankful to have collared. But if *you* are unfaithful to *him*, he's a poor worm.

Haven't men arranged this neatly? And isn't it unfair to women?

Men have also unfortunately managed to establish that they are polygamous—whereas girls are only interested in 'the one and only' man in their lives. And they've got the girls to believe them.

All this makes it a bad idea to repay unfaithfulness with unfaithfulness. It just starts a vicious circle in which each keeps on trying to hit harder than the other.

i. & s.h.

Something is Missing

I'm a married woman of thirty-five, and I find it very hard to pull myself together to write to you about my problem.

My problem is that I never feel sort of 'all set' to make love. I never feel what men call randy—which I think is an unfortunate word for it. It must be so lovely to look forward to it and feel your blood rushing and surging through your veins the way one so often reads about. Do you think I'll ever experience it?

I must mention that I have orgasms and all that at quite regular intervals. I've got a wonderful husband and he sees to that all right, but I would so like to feel the urge myself sometimes.

It's a problem many women have to contend with. By the way, men don't feel the Mighty Urge coursing through their veins every time either. But women do seem to have a few more inhibitions.

Many women are capable of feeling sexual excitement beforehand, and most of them are at least able to notice something of the sort at the beginning of a relationship. It's more difficult in the course of the daily round of married life, what with disappointments of one kind and another, children needing to have buttons sewn on and all the other things that make a housewife feel she's seldom allowed a proper day off.

But we know of cases of women who only began feeling 'all set to make love' (as you put it) when they got into their fifties—

also of cases of women who had their first orgasms with a man when they were about this age. It'll come all right.

i. & s.h.

Spring Cleaning

Can a woman be called abnormal if she avoids sexual relations with her husband as much as possible simply because he's a pig— minus the grunts? Changes his underwear without having a bath first, etc.?

I close my eyes and pretend to be asleep. I dream of a clean, kind husband instead.

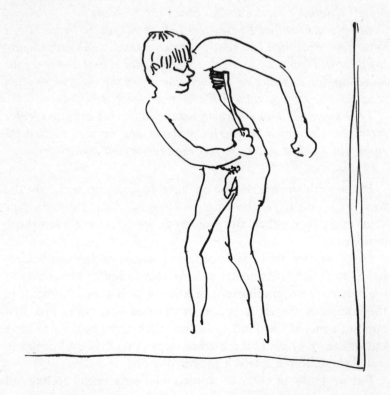

You're touching a sore point there. An awful lot of men never stop to think that ingrained dirt and dried sweat aren't exactly inspiring to their wives. We'd like to state that we agree with you completely.

Having said this much—and without detracting from it in the slightest—we must also mention that there *are* women who use it as an excuse—an excuse to avoid having sexual relations. There's just a hint of this in your letter when you write: 'I dream about a clean, *kind* . . .' It's possible you will defend your position by saying he's not only dirty but he's not a nice chap either. But you probably understand what we're getting at.

And finally we'd certainly like to return to the main point and say that seeing most women find it so hard to be as keen on sexual intercourse as their husbands, perhaps this could be an additional incentive to men to make themselves more appetizing?

How about showing him this?

i. & s.h.

Harem

Here's a problem which I don't think can be very common—or is it? My husband admitted the other day (under pressure) that he is still fond of a spot of variation where girls are concerned. This

confession was made after we'd been married for barely twelve months and as a result of the fact that I discovered he'd been going to bed with a female colleague whom he brought home and introduced me to a long time ago and actually encouraged me to make friends with. It was rather a bitter pill to have to swallow— thinking back to the little tête-à-têtes she and I have had in the evenings sometimes, when I dare say I must have confided various things to her. I bet she thought it was funny. Having recovered from the shock I've been wondering what the reason for this taste for variation can be. It certainly can't be because of a boring sex life, as we're both very erotic by nature, we make love together often, in all sorts of ways and invariably to the complete satisfaction of both of us.

My husband says he can't promise not to have the odd little fling, and as he has a job which involves a lot of travelling he has plenty of opportunities. He just can't understand my point of view at all. After all, I'm the one he loves and the one he wanted to have for a wife.

Can one get used to an attitude like his? Should I leave him before we have any children? Is he mentally deranged? Or is it me who's abnormal because I happen to think I'm monogamous?

PS. He wouldn't like me to behave the same way.

Perhaps ninety-nine per cent of women could have written what you have written. Men love the myth that they are polygamous—and they love trying to convince their wives that women aren't.

We live in a patriarchy in which men's ideas have impressed themselves on both men and women. Men write most of the pornography too—look at the way pornographic books are full of superstition about sex life.

Well, we just want to say that men and women naturally think that persons other than their lawfully wedded wives/ husbands are exciting. Mature men and women can control their desire to find out just *how* exciting they are—or they can come to a gentlemen's agreement to the effect that they're *both* free to do so. Immature men do what your husband is doing!

We're talking about the present, because we believe that moral attitudes will become a bit more elastic in time. But both you and we were brought up under a stricter code, so we can't very well relax our demands.

In other words, we don't think you're monogamous, but that your husband and society have fooled you into believing you are!

So you're entitled to claim equal rights.

i. & s.h.

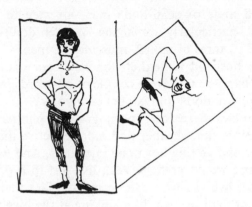

He's Got Nudes in His Pocket

I feel a bit embarrassed about writing to you about this, but on the other hand I need somebody's advice. I'm twenty-four years of age, have been married for almost five years, and we've got a little boy aged four. I've always thought we were a happy family, but the other day I discovered something which made me wonder.

I was going to brush my husband's jacket and was going to see if it needed mending anywhere, when I found some pornographic pictures in his pocket, pictures of girls in the nude, or semi-nude, wearing black suspender belts and that sort of tarty thing. I haven't said anything to him about having seen them, and I don't know whether I ought to, or just try to forget about it, even though it's hard. What do you think?

We think you ought to buy yourself a black suspender belt as fast as possible! Well, we don't mean it quite that crudely, but —why can't lawfully wedded wives be a bit gay and tarty to look at on festive occasions, when they're *alone* with their husbands? It's your plain duty! Now we're joking again, but there really is something in it. (See the Consumer Guide at the end of this book.)

Most men think pictures of semi-nude girls are exciting and fun to look at. This is a fact that should neither startle nor shock you. Very few women can understand it, because very few women find nude or semi-nude men—or men in long black underpants—particularly appetizing. Women don't buy magazines full of pictures of naked, muscular he-men.

But your husband is neither abnormal nor dissatisfied just because he happens to have a couple of postcards in his pocket —what were you doing in his pocket anyway?

Pornographic magazines, pornographic photos and dirty books are more fun, cheaper and more effective than going to see a doctor and getting hormone injections. And we're certain your husband would prefer a real, live girl to a postcard any time—a real, live girl who can accept the fact that men, to a greater extent than women, like looking at the lovely creatures.

i. & s.h.

No Time for Love

My husband and I are the same age, but there the similarity ends. He's full of energy, always pushing ahead. He's got a flair for business and the gift of the gab, and according to him—and also others—he has brought off hundreds of erotic conquests. I had to hear all about these and 'forgive him his sins'. In the beginning he more or less worshipped me because I was his ideal, pure and innocent and all that, but I wasn't interested in that sort of thing.

I was rather cautious, and it was not until we'd known each other for three months that 'intimacy took place' between us as they say. We both come from 'respectable' families, but made no secret of the fact that we'd started living together—as far as was possible.

Being rather slenderly built (at least I think so!) I had a lot of difficulty getting used to our sexual relations in the beginning, but my fiancé was terribly understanding and we had a marvellous time for a year or so, until we decided to get married.

And then the difficulties started. All of a sudden my husband— on account of his work and many other things—just didn't have the surplus energy to have anything to do with me sexually, not so much as a kiss or a pat, let alone actually sleeping with me. It was rather an abrupt change, and during the years that have passed since then I've been racking my brains to work out what can have caused the transformation.

My first reaction, when it started, was that we shouldn't get married after all. But he insisted, and so—well, one has heard of men getting into a bit of a nervous state in this situation, and so we got married after all. To begin with we lived in a terrible place, but now we've got a lovely modern flat. I've tried going on strike and moving into a little room of my own. I've also tried all sorts of things like black underwear, transparent nighties, surprise attacks and serious discussions, but all to no avail.

A wise old doctor suggested, as a last resort, having a baby. I'm now pregnant and realize that this last attempt has misfired too. My husband will be a splendid father but remains an emotionally and erotically hopeless husband. So now I ask you, can you give me any advice?

I'm not a prude and I haven't tried to force things.

Is there anything else at all I can try?

I've never tried going to bed with other men, and have no desire to do so. I must stop here—I'll have to go and get myself another big pocket handkerchief!

Despite the length of your letter (which we've shortened a bit here), you don't say in what way your husband excuses himself —what he says when you have your serious talks.

It is very seldom in a marriage that both partners feel they make love together often enough. As a rule it's the husband who is dissatisfied, but in your case, you are the one who is impatient.

There could be many reasons why your husband has been put 'out of action'—or become less interested.

You may have taken him by surprise and hurt his feelings. Men are terribly vain, and 'hundreds' of erotic conquests at his age points to a lack of sexual confidence that needs repeated bolstering. But it might be something else.

Studying hard can be a form of pressure that reduces the sexual urge—so can financial or other worries. Or he may have become less fond of you—or more fond of another girl.

These are all matters about which you can do very little.

As a matter of fact, *he* is the one who needs advice and help. Can't you get him to go to somebody or other in whom he has confidence?

i. & s.h.

PS. I don't suppose he's got any silly ideas about the woman he loves being too 'pure' for sex, has he?

RSVP

1. I'm past forty and would like to know if a woman's clitoris disappears with the years.

2. I'd also like to know if it does any harm to play with yourself a bit.

3. Is it harmful to go without sex for several months? Does it reduce potency?

Plain questions! We'll try to make our answers equally plain.

1. No, fortunately a woman's clitoris does not disappear with the years. (Did you know, by the way, that in large parts of the Arab world, 'female circumcision' is practised on all young girls, i.e. the clitoris is removed by an operation? As a result, it is very difficult for them to get anything out of their sex lives.)

2. Of course it isn't the slightest bit harmful to 'play with

oneself'—to masturbate. People thought it was in the old days, but it's pure nonsense. It doesn't matter whether you masturbate a little or a lot, it's still completely harmless.

3. Nobody goes without sex in some form or other 'for months'. There are and have always been religious fanatics who try to escape 'the lusts of the flesh', and in some cases they have been seen to go crazy in the attempt. But no doubt their self-assumed feeling of guilt has been the cause. If by 'sex' you mean sexual intercourse with another person, well, it's rather dull to go without it for months on end, but not downright harmful.

i. & s.h.

It's All Right for Men . . .

Not so long ago I read in one of your columns about a soldier stationed in Cyprus who suggested that brothels should be provided for soldiers during the six months' spell of duty they do on the island—rather than risk catching a venereal disease from casual pick-ups.

I understand him so well.

I presume a number of these soldiers are married or have a fiancée at home. What about her? She might feel like being with a man during the time he's away too. Is this acceptable?

I am, of course, a woman.

Thank you for your letter. You raise an important point.

If we're to be completely fair, it is probably true that going without sex is a slightly bigger problem for the majority of men than it is for the majority of women. But this also means, putting it another way, that it can be more difficult for some women.

And probably the majority of women feel just as great a need to be together with another person—to cuddle, dance and have fun.

i. & s.h.

Filthy?

I'm a young woman of forty-two and unmarried. Recently I've got to know a man of fifty-eight. He's not interested in sleeping with me, but just wants me to kiss his private parts.
I think it's filthy, and so our relationship looks like breaking up. Can you give me any good advice?

We can. But will you take it? First we'd like to praise you for calling yourself a young woman of forty-two. Far too many women say they feel old at that age—which is all wrong. In the case of many, many women, life—and sex life in particular—begins after forty. So you're quite right.

But you're not right to call what he has proposed 'filthy'. Perhaps you have been brought up to regard sex as filthy. Your parents were brought up by parents who had learnt that sex was something you indulged in to have children.

We're sure you'll agree that's all nonsense.

We're equally sure we can't convince you just by saying you're wrong and he's right.

But you might like to think it over?

We can only add that if he fondles your sensitive parts first—we're thinking here of the sexual organs and perhaps the breasts—in such a way as to stimulate you, preferably until you are sexually satisfied, i.e. have an orgasm—then you might make him happy in the same way.

And then you and he, together, would have discovered something which many couples have taken years to work out between them.

It's a very effective, pleasant and satisfying form of sexual togetherness—one that is neither perverse, revolting nor the slightest bit unusual.

i. & s.h.

An Old Dog

When my husband and I met each other five years ago I was young and completely inexperienced. My husband, though, who is much older than me, had lived a gay and exciting life with any number of mistresses and girl-friends. I was so impressed by all his adventures that I became completely obsessed by him.

Now, after five years' marriage, I feel slightly cheated. He has taught me to be the perfect mistress—so he says—but what about me? He thinks he satisfies me sexually because he's quite nicely equipped physically, but I keep begging and imploring him to do something else that I would find more exciting. But he won't. He says I'm perverted. What shall I do? I love my husband, and we get on fine together otherwise. Sometimes I do have an orgasm, but it's relatively seldom.

As often as I can, I try to explain to him what it is I would like. I recommend him erotic books, thinking he might learn something from them, but he only gets hurt and offended at my suggesting that I haven't enjoyed myself in bed with him.

All the other women he used to know 'thought he was fantastic'. He really believes it! He may be a proper Don Juan, but I think he's a very narrow-minded one.

I've thought of being unfaithful to him, thinking it might rouse him, but I haven't got the courage—or the desire—for I really do love him. I think he loves me too, but perhaps he's too old. I'm twenty-six, he's forty-two. Do you think one can teach an old dog new tricks?

Well, anyway—no matter how dearly I love my husband, I don't love him dearly enough to keep on like this. My sex life means too much to me. Unfortunately I don't think anyone can help me, but now at least I've let off a bit of steam.

We've had any number of letters from women whose husbands think they themselves are fantastic and that it's a woman's plain duty to be grateful to the god-like creature she's managed to get hold of. These men have completely false but widespread male notions about what it takes to be a good lover.

'All the other girls—
all of them, I tell you
—have been *so*
grateful!'

They attach importance to quite the wrong things instead of trying to learn something about what actually interests women in the sphere of sexual relationships.

Women are *not* interested in bulging sexual athletes who can bounce up and down for hours on end.

Men like this should just listen to what mature, experienced women say about them, day after day. They'd be *astonished* if they ever realized how many of the women they had known had simulated pleasure, pretended to be having feelings they never really had at all.

One of the dreadful things about this business of pretending is that the men who have been deceived in this way later entertain their wives with stories about the grateful girls they used to know. Women who simulate sexual pleasure not only let themselves down and deceive their husbands; they let down all womankind.

It may sound as if we haven't answered your question. But we have. We want to bolster up your self-confidence, so that you'll feel strong enough to grab the old fathead by the scruff of his neck and the seat of his pants and give him a piece of your mind.

i. & s.h.

I Pretend

I'm a young girl of nineteen. I hope you can help me with a problem which seems to be looming bigger and bigger before me.

I've been going to bed with my fiancé for a year or so. But although I'm terribly fond of him, I don't feel anything when we make love together.

As we don't live in the same town, we can't meet as often as we'd like to, so I can't help thinking about how things will work out when we get married, which will be quite soon. I can't tell my fiancé, because it would make him terribly unhappy, but on the other hand, will I be able to go on pretending?

Is there anything a doctor could give me that would help? I'm not thinking of giving him up on this account for one moment, because I love him, and I'm still clinging to the hope that it may yet be possible to find an answer to this big problem of mine.

I refuse to believe I'm frigid.

You're a stout-hearted girl, and we take our hats off to you.

You mustn't despair or give up, because it'll all come right in time. But you're going to have to work hard for it. A happy sex life doesn't just come wandering along by itself. It doesn't come to any woman as a matter of course—it's only men who are fortunate in this way.

It takes years to build up a good sexual relationship. And it demands peaceful, pleasant living conditions, something which engaged couples seldom have—and unfortunately the same goes for many married couples.

Above all it demands *cooperation*.

So we're sure you'll understand that you've got to stop pretending.

Men are terribly vain—particularly about their sexual relationships—so you're right when you say it'll be a hard blow for him. But he could take it today. But not when you've been chewing your eiderdown for ten or twenty years.

You must let him read your letter and our answer, and he is very welcome to write to us too. You and he must study the latest books on sexual relationships together. We can recommend, for example, Albert Ellis's books.

In the old days it was believed that anybody could solve this sort of problem all by himself (or herself). Today some people are wiser.

i. & s.h.

I Could Scream

I'm divorced and have a little boy aged eight. About eighteen months ago I married a bachelor of about thirty-two. About ten years ago he was engaged for three years or so. But her family didn't think he was good enough.

We met and got married after only four months. Everything was lovely and straightforward, including our sex life. As a rule we slept together two or three times a week. We always had a nice time, but somehow we never really achieved what you might call the real thing. In the course of a few months my husband withdrew from me—I mean, since October last year he hasn't slept in our bedroom at all, but in the living-room.

We both wanted to have a child, but he couldn't understand why it didn't happen as soon as we'd made up our minds. I went and saw a doctor last summer, but it didn't help. Just after New Year I went to see him again, and I told him that our sexual relationship wasn't too good. He said he'd like to talk to my husband, who went and saw him a month later, and he was given five hormone injections at fortnightly intervals. He didn't have the sixth one. He said he wasn't going any more, because they didn't help.

In the beginning I didn't understand why he didn't want to have anything to do with me. In some respects he's very impatient, perhaps in this respect too. He works rather hard, and sometimes takes on a bit extra in the evenings. The doctor said he was probably working too hard. And then he worries, and crosses a good many bridges before he comes to them, so to speak. But he's kind to my boy and thinks of his future and always mends his bicycle for him, and let's him help with interesting tasks.

I knew he had a lot of things to think about, and so I pretended to take no notice for a few months. We've talked about it, but he just dismisses it, and sometimes he says it's no use because we're not 'sexually compatible'. I've been given nerve pills and then sleeping pills afterwards, but I have to take two or three if I want to sleep all night, otherwise I keep thinking about it the whole time, and often cry. I get headaches and can taste the pills the whole of the next day. I work in an office during the daytime and feel awful there too. I'm getting completely desperate about all this. I'm very fond of my husband and respect him and admire him in many ways. I think he's fond of me too, though he hasn't said so for the past year. We kiss each other, but he never makes any attempt to go any further, and if I do he gets angry, and so I've given up trying.

I long for him so desperately when he comes home in the afternoon at four-thirty, but I'm afraid of the evening too. It just sort of tears at my insides when I say good-night and go to bed with a paper, a book and a couple of sleeping pills.

I've tried going without pills, but then I only sleep for two or

*three hours and feel terribly tired the next day. My husband thinks
I should go and see a doctor. He thinks I must be ill if I always
keep on having these headaches.*

*I do so badly wish we could make things go right again, but
how? The last time I saw our doctor he told me he'd speak to a
specialist my husband could go and see, but my husband won't.
He's fully convinced that I'm the one there's something the matter
with.*

*We've both read sex books, but it's not much help when there's
no chance of my husband wanting to sleep with me. I'm willing to
try anything to make things go right, and I think my husband
would too, really, but something seems to be preventing him—
what can it be? Otherwise we have a nice time together, and have
fun, but he goes all silent and peculiar if once in a while (it's very
seldom now) I steer the conversation round to this delicate subject.*

*All the people in the area where we live are young couples with
prams and tricycles in the garden, the wives go round with bulging
tummies, and I get quite sick with the thought that we can't have
a baby. I get all tied up inside, and look the other way.*

*My husband doesn't understand why I burst into tears some-
times, and gets irritated if I say there's nothing the matter.*

*I know my husband would like to have a little girl, and in fact
he's said we'll have one some day. But what am I supposed to
believe? After all, the storks don't bring them. I've tried to keep
the house and our clothes and myself clean and decent, but
sometimes I feel it's all pointless, especially the bedroom, where
he never comes except to change into nice clothes. Well no, he
comes along every morning and calls me when he's made the coffee
and boiled the eggs. Sometimes I feel as though I could scream,
but I never show it.*

The situation you describe in your letter is a very serious one.
We fully understand that you are desperate and that something
must be done. The way you present the case, it's clearly up to
your husband to do something. He cannot merely insist that you
are the one who needs adjusting. But of course it is very seldom
exclusively the fault of the one person or the other when a

relationship finds itself up a blind alley. An interplay must take place between the two persons concerned in any human relationship, and it *is* possible for one partner to thrust the other away. Most men are very vain where sexual matters are concerned, and your husband is moreover impatient and easily hurt and, as you say, tends to cross his bridges before he comes to them.

It doesn't sound too good, for as a rule it is the man who needs to take the initiative if a sexual relationship is to develop in the right direction.

But now you're the one that has to keep on trying to get things moving in this respect. It requires tact, patience and love— perhaps more than it would be reasonable to ask.

As you say, babies aren't brought along by storks, so in a way your husband's and your wish to have a child together comes into the picture. Still, you had better regard this matter independently of your sexual relations together. The child shouldn't become something that is going to save your marriage. A child can't do this—and it shouldn't be the driving force behind your wish to patch up your relations with your husband.

Do you think you could find an opportunity to fix a nice, cosy little dinner just for your husband and yourself? Without children, and with a spot of beer or wine or whatever you feel might help to break the ice? Serve his favourite dish and put on a pretty dress, powder your nose and do your hair the way he likes it best.

And then, afterwards, sit down with him and ask him to read your letter and our answer.

Try to get him to understand that this is really serious. That you love and admire him and have arranged all this in an attempt to break the deadlock in which you find yourselves. That he is only alienating himself from his wife and her son more and more with every day that passes—even if he does have close daily contact with them. You *must* force your way through to him and have a not too desperate showdown with him—even if you *are* desperate.

He must go to see a proper specialist. Unfortunately most doctors don't know so very much about sexual relationships, but a doctor would be in a position to put your husband on to somebody who could help him if your attempt isn't enough to bring you together again.

Reading books *may* help, but then reading doesn't always amount to the same as understanding. And where sex is concerned, we all look at things through coloured spectacles. The result is that we have to read and read and discuss things again and again—before things really penetrate and become properly understood.

And then there's still a way to go, because you can understand something with your intellect, but that isn't enough. You also have to understand it with your emotions. So you have a long and difficult path ahead of you. It's easier if you can tackle it *with* your husband. He simply must understand this.

Otherwise you'll go on being the two silly separate halves of a marriage.

Life is too lovely and too short for that.

i. & s.h.

Widespread Superstition

There's one thing I'd very much like you to answer.

I'm going very steady with a marvellous man. We're not engaged and we don't live together, but almost. We get on well, very well indeed, sexually. In fact it gets better and better. It's lasted almost eighteen months now. But here comes the 'problem'. I've never tried having an orgasm in my vagina. This doesn't worry me, but my boy-friend is unhappy about it and thinks he's an oaf. I've assured him that 'all' the girls he's been with and he claims have had vaginal orgasms must either be good actresses or very rare birds. Of course it would be very nice, but it's not as if it were that important. Nor does it matter that much whether I have an orgasm every time or not—but gosh, do I enjoy it! When I do have an orgasm he's certainly never left in any doubt about it. None of your petty little twitches, but the really big nerve-shattering moment that defies description. And to think I should have been married for nine years and divorced for four before I experienced it!

Well, that's beside the point. But would you please be so kind as to reassure my sweetheart that nothing's the matter? I don't want to have him doubting the excellence of his talents.

We're delighted to have your letter. It gives us an opportunity to thoroughly squash a foolish and persistent superstition.

You say in your letter that you've never tried having an orgasm in the vagina itself. Well, nor has any other woman! But it's a widespread superstition among men. And to suggest that such a thing as a *vaginal orgasm* exists is, as we say, a silly superstition.

It's a silly superstition because it's filled hundreds of thousands of women with inferiority complexes, because they've worried about the fact that they have 'only' had *clitoral orgasms*. All women achieve sexual satisfaction through titillation of the little button just above the entrance to the vagina. It's the button that switches on the pleasurable feelings, and it's called a *clitoris*. But ignorant men and submissive women have used, for many years, tons and tons of energy in quite the wrong places. Lovely, sweet, warm-blooded, delightful girls have thought something was missing.

Unfortunately very, very few people—and only the most recent of books on sexual enlightenment—are aware of this misunderstanding. To ditch this superstition would bring about a revolution—and a happier state of affairs—in the majority of marriages.

Most men believe it's something any fool can work out. But they can't! We congratulate your boy-friend on having you.

i. & s.h.

Can't be Bothered

My husband feels he wants to make love to me two or three times a week, but he just doesn't grasp the fact that I need to be warmed up a bit first.

He warms himself up until he's got an erection. Then he gets cracking—and, as you can imagine, it doesn't take him long before he's finished.

I've tried talking to him about it many times, but it never does any good. On the contrary, he hints that I must be perverted. I can't be bothered any more.

So I manage by myself instead. I masturbate, and get a lovely orgasm out of it. So I have a nice time by myself, but I miss having somebody else to have a nice time with.

I would so like him to kiss my clitoris: it's something you have mentioned a few times, and I'm beginning to wonder if I should find a man—or perhaps a woman—who would understand me better and whom I could make happy and satisfied too.

What do you advise me to do, or do you think it's dreadful of me?

We've had many letter like yours, and it's a sad state of affairs. On principle, we feel you should give your husband a chance or two to wake up, but we also realize there unfortunately still exist ignorant and unsympathetic men whom it's almost impossible to rouse into changing their ways.

It can prove necessary to give men of this kind a real fright—by leaving them, for instance. It may be about the only thing likely to give their bone-headed male self-righteousness a shaking-up. But it isn't easy.

It's astonishing that in this year of our Lord—or the Devil—
and right in the middle of an era of pornography and sex, too—
so much stubborn, blind ignorance should still exist. But then
much pornographic literature is only very slightly *informative*,
but aims more at being *stimulative*. (And here, as in all other
spheres, the truth is far less exciting than a lie.)

We understand you so well.

i. & s.h.

Ladies First?

. *I'm sick and tired of hearing about all these considerate men
who hold back. 'And then he has an ejaculation, but never before
he's sure I've come.' Bah!*

*When I meet a gentleman in a doorway and he politely steps
back and says 'Ladies first!', I always find myself thinking of my
sex life.*

· *I'm twenty-five and have known my husband for nine years, and
my God, am I tired of coming first! I've told him so. Variety is the
spice of life, they say, don't they? It gives me complexes having to
lie there wondering whether I'm taking too long to come.*

*It so happens I'm just not interested in the hard weapon anyway
—on the contrary. Just after he's ejaculated, when it's sort of
thick and floppy, that's how I like it. Then I can relax and come.*

You've got some problems, and we're sure many people will
be glad to hear about them. We think you touch on a very
important point—and it's so good when women do this.

We too would like to help change the misunderstood form of
potency worship—change the old, strenuous concept of potency
into a more relaxed kind that takes the woman's wishes and
ideas into consideration to a much larger extent.

Many of those who read your letter will find it a relief to hear
you speak up and say how you would like things. We quite agree
with you.

i. & s.h.

Twelve-Year-Old Men

What on earth shall I do? It came out because my husband and I had been reading your column together. Suddenly he tells me his biggest wish is for me to hit him when we're in bed together. He wants to be my naughty little boy and I'm to be a stern lady who punishes him.

I've tried doing it, but I don't like it. I want a proper grown-up man, not a whimpering baby. I've lost all my respect for him—or practically.

We must speak to you harshly. You've been going round clinging to a few ideals about people—ideals that just won't hold when it comes to the point.

You use a sentence we often hear: 'I want a proper grown-up man.' It's tragic to think that men go round pretending to be strong and masculine—and women pretending to be small and fragile. Both start off aiming at something like a father-daughter relationship in which the husband is the tender protector who shoulders the responsibilities, and the wife is a weak little ninny. These are the rôles which society has told men and women to play—but they aren't the rôles we were born to play.

Most women wake up with a jerk after their marriage and realize that these traditional rôles are just a superstition that has been imposed upon us. It may happen after they've been married only a short while, or it may take twenty years before it suddenly dawns on them. I thought I'd married a *man*, a proper, grown-up man—but he's only a child!

Let's get something quite straight. Emotionally men seldom get to be any older than eight—or twelve at most.

You may smile, but it's true. In a way, women are more grown-up and mature than their husbands. And this isn't just the exception—it's the rule! Like so many other girls, you have put your husband on a pedestal where he never belonged. You've read about men who were men. You've seen them in films and you've met proper he-men in the streets and at parties. Of course you have.

But do you know what the wives of all these he-men are afraid of? That other people may discover that their he-men are just little boys in reality. Let's put it another way. If two people are going to have a nice time together, they must be able to relax in each other's company. They must be able to lean on each other for support, and be honest with each other both in happiness and unhappiness. They must be capable of being human beings together—without paying any attention to the rôles which society happens to have given them to play.

The best thing would be if you could accept your husband as he is—including the little preference he has mentioned. But, of course, you can't force yourself to do so.

There's another thing which is just as important. How much do *you* get out of your marital relations?

If *you* get full satisfaction and have *your* little whims fulfilled, then there's a far greater chance of your being in a position to regard *his* little whims with more leniency. You scratch my back and I'll scratch yours!

i. & s.h.

Only Once

How can it be that my husband, who was born in 1938, is only able to make love once every time we sleep together? It worries him a great deal, but, as I tell him, if we both get a lot of pleasure out of it, even if it is only once, then what does it matter?

Can there be any special reason for it? Is it because he works too hard? Is there anything I can do to help him?

The year 1938 was a very fine one. All men can manage only once—and then they have to have a little pause before the next round. And the pause gets longer and longer with the years. Just reassure your husband by telling him that he's like the rest of the 1938 vintage—and that they, just like him, were able to start again a bit faster ten years ago.

But we have no doubt he's both kinder and more skilful than

most twenty-year-olds, and than he was himself at the age of twenty.

Women, on the other hand, can certainly learn to have a second orgasm right on top of the first—without having to pause for breath. This is one of the differences between the sexes that the American research team Masters and Johnson have proved.

But the important thing is that your husband ought to get away from his silly male vanity and instead be happy about what his sensible wife so rightly says.

i. & s.h.

The Male Change of Life

My husband and I are going to be divorced.

We've been married for twenty years. There's never been any great passion between us. In recent years, in particular, our sexual relations have practically faded out altogether.

Even so, we have so many ties, including the business which we have built up together and which provides us with all our material needs plus a bit more—so our marriage is actually both a good and sound one.

We've both tried going off on our own, and have shown mutual understanding for each other's escapades. It's not that we've ever had any clear agreement about it, but it has more or less been in the air.

But I'm not going to be understanding any more now.

A couple of months ago my husband met a woman of about his own age in Tenerife and spent his entire holiday with her. She hadn't much money herself, so he hired a car and took her round the island, out to dinner and to night-clubs. Just as if she was his wife, and hand in hand like a couple of youngsters, they amused each other by relating their experiences in their respective marriages and discussed their mutual interest in diseases.

But they never went to bed together.

My husband's sexual unfaithfulness has never worried me, nor have I felt that mine has deprived him of anything. But this mental

*unfaithfulness has hurt me badly. He has transferred to another
woman the confidence he normally reserves for me.*

*She has even given him various bits of advice about his and my
sex life. A great deal of it concerns things I told my husband long
ago, though without ever being able to persuade him to try. Now
he is trying to persuade me to take her advice. This is rather more
than I can stick.*

*All other kinds of unfaithfulness have never bothered me. But
this time he has found somebody who can replace me, and this is
the kind of unfaithfulness which I regard as really serious. We are
now heading towards divorce.*

PS. *We are trying to save what we can from the wreck.*
PPS. *Is it the fact that I am approaching the change of life that
makes me particularly touchy?*
PPPS. *Am I being unfair to him?*

Um. It's not easy to save bits and pieces from a wreck.

It's a bit late to raise a moralizing finger, but we'd like to
remind you and others that a lasting marriage isn't something
one *has*. It's something you have to fight for every single day.
We all forget this.

You have built up a secure, good marriage, you write, and of
course it is possible to live quite a nice and tolerable existence
together in holy, or unholy, wedlock—even without a mutual
erotic interest—though this is more difficult.

In addition, you and your husband are now approaching the
dangerous age, usually during one's forties, when one starts
examining one's whole life with an embarrassingly critical eye.
And men are particularly bad about this.

'How many of those things I dreamt about as a boy have I
actually achieved?' a man asks himself. 'I'm going to have this
wife for the rest of my life, this furniture, this job, these children.
I shall go on living in this same street,' he says, and glances
round appraisingly.

Women of the kind your husband has taken up with are the
most dangerous, as you very rightly sense. The domestic helps

who do their consoling horizontally aren't nearly as serious a threat as the ones who wander round and hold hands.

If at this point you interrupt us and say 'Thank you very much, that was an *analysis* of my problems, but what am I to *do*?' we have to admit you are completely right. It's easier to analyse the case than to advise you. The chances aren't very great.

You could take him by the scruff of the neck and the seat of the pants and chuck him out—kindly but firmly. Just for a month. And still hope that you and he have, after all, so many ties that he will come back to the fold on his hands and knees. This would be the most violent solution—and the best—but it may be difficult for a number of practical reasons.

The next best thing is to discuss matters frankly, trying to understand and accept each other's weaknesses, and carefully plan an attempt to heal the few nasty gashes your marriage has sustained.

Not many people will believe it, but it is very often precisely between the ages of forty and fifty that a good marital sex life can be developed.

It is by no means too late.

i. & s.h.

High Tension

My husband works abroad, and as we have children attending school it is impossible for us to be together. Unfortunately I'm a very warm-blooded girl and produce a lot of hormones I can't properly get rid of. Masturbation is of course a solution that eases the pressure a bit, but it isn't enough.

Now I've met a woman who is sweet and talented, but a little shy. When we meet at a party you can practically see little electric sparks flying between us. I get very nearly panicky at the thought that a woman can make such a strong impression on me. Especially as I get on wonderfully with my husband—sexually as well.

I'd like to know if one can suddenly change one's outlook? Does it mean that, without being conscious of it before, I've always really wanted a homosexual relationship? Or am I going out of my mind?

What about an electric vibrator? What do they look like and how do you use them? Where can you buy them?

I hope an apparatus of this kind can help me to get through some of my fantasies so that I can recover my good humour and receive my husband with a clear conscience when he comes home for a while this winter.

Well, it sounds as though things are getting a bit urgent.

It seems to us as if the best solution would be if your husband found work at home, or if you took the children abroad with you and put them in a school there. But of course there may be circumstances which prevent it. Incidentally, how do you think your husband is coping with his corresponding problem?

Perhaps a good deal could be clarified and solved if you and he could have a proper chat about it? But of course that too depends on a number of factors of which we have no knowledge.

An electric vibrator is a good way of obtaining an orgasm. They are usually obtainable in shops that sell sun lamps and surgical appliances—or they can be ordered through the post from specialist firms. Most of them can be used provided there is a spinning extension that can titillate the woman's clitoris. Tastes and needs differ, so we can't recommend any particular type.

But an electric vibrator won't satisfy your natural need and desire to have some form of sexual intercourse with another person.

You haven't changed your outlook, nor do you have any marked homosexual tendency that need scare you. You are merely—if we may borrow a phrase from another sphere of bodily need—pretty ravenous, which means there are a good many more things that could satisfy your appetite than some luxurious food. If you're really starving, a stale crust and a bit of dog food can be lovely too—not that we want to suggest any comparison with your girl friend!

We think you'll understand what we mean. Necessity is the mother of invention, they say—and we believe this is more or less your situation.

But give a thought to our first suggestion!

i. & s.h.

Fight for Everything

I've got the most wonderful husband in the world. He helps me and is kind to me in every way, but he's half Spanish and very, very hot-blooded. I can tell you, things really do boil.

The problem has come up because when we go to bed together he uses his fingers before doing the proper thing. I put up with it until a couple of months ago. Then I told him I wasn't going to have it. And then he said, it's just as much for your sake as for mine. And if you forbid me to do it, there's not much point in my being here.

I replied that I thought he was a filthy swine and that I simply wouldn't have it. I ought never to have said it, because every time I can tell it's about the time he'd like to go to bed with me, he just isn't at home at night any more. And I know what he's up to.

I've tried talking to him, but he just looks at me without saying a word.

I've also talked to one of my girl-friends, who's been to bed with him too, but she says I've been very silly. And that lots of girls would envy me, because he's really the perfect husband.

I fully realize this. All the girls used to be after him. But I'm a little bit afraid of him too, because sometimes he can make me so excited, and so worked up, that I almost feel I'm in a sort of lovely hypnotic trance—and it scares me.

What shall I do now? I do miss him so dreadfully.

Yes, you have been a silly little goof—to be quite blunt about it. But it's no earthly use our trampling triumphantly all over you, because it's not your fault you were brought up with a narrow-minded, prudish outlook on these matters—or that you haven't managed to extricate yourself from it yet.

It's your parents' fault—and that's nonsense too, for they are also merely the results of the upbringing they were given.

You don't say how old you are, but you sound very young and naïve.

Let us correct a couple of misunderstandings. Your half-Spanish husband has no hotter blood in his veins than the majority of other men. It is possible, however, that he has been given a little more opportunity to display his temperament. His finger technique isn't particularly Spanish.

But he sounds quite sensible. For it's wise of him to 'warm you up' first. Very few women are able to derive much enjoyment from sexual intercourse if the man just inserts his penis and starts flopping up and down.

You say you get carried away by your passion, but you don't mention whether you actually manage to have an orgasm. We have a faint suspicion that you don't—in which case his finger technique isn't all that good—perhaps he doesn't keep it up long enough.

It sounds as if he has grasped something of the truth about women's sexual satisfaction, but not quite all of it. And this is perhaps where part of your problem lies—something that you and he ought to try to solve together.

He's not the slightest bit 'filthy'. *You* have been a prudish cissy—admittedly through no fault of your own, but you've also clung to your middle-class morality and thereby made it more difficult for him.

You say it scares you to find he is capable of exciting you so much sexually. And this is another aspect of the problem. Many women are afraid of their own feelings, of floating away, of losing their grip on themselves, of losing consciousness, and so forth.

The anxiety is there, and it's not enough to say 'Nonsense, stop it!' On the other hand it's not right to succumb to this anxiety and give up either. Most women must be prepared to put up a fight if they want to get anything out of their sex lives.

Show him your letter and our answer and then have a good old chat to him about the whole thing. Promise him you'll make an effort, but at the same time ask him to be patient and persevering. You'll succeed all right—if you both try together.

i. & s.h.

I've Given Up!

Time and again you keep telling women who don't get anything out of their sexual relationships that 'it'll come all right in time'. Why do you never write about those to whom it never does come? But perhaps you've never heard about them?

I'm thirty-nine, and I've given up. I've been to see doctors and I've read any number of books, but with no result. I got a grant to go and see a psychoanalyst, but all we did was talk.

I'm quite sexy and actually enjoy sexual intercourse, but I miss that finishing touch, so to speak. Am I frigid?

I can't just pretend to be having an orgasm either—for one thing because I don't know how a woman behaves with a man when she's having one.

So now I've just given up, because it never happens anyway, no matter what is done to me.

No, fortunately you haven't given up, or you wouldn't have bothered to write to us. We say fortunately because there's still hope.

You don't say whether you're married, nor do you tell us if you've ever had an orgasm through masturbation, or dreams. We've never met a woman who didn't have an orgasm in some way or other. And the two American sexologists, Masters and Johnson, state that the kind of orgasm you have by yourself, i.e. without sexual intercourse or the help of another person, is in a way the best—from the point of view of 'quality'.

But of course you would naturally like to experience having an orgasm with somebody else. The same applies to most people, and most people do experience it sooner or later. But there are women who reach the age of forty, fifty and even sixty before they succeed. It is seldom it takes so long before a woman finds the technique and the understanding kind of man who's prepared to spend the necessary amount of time on 'warming her up'—but of course there are cases.

We understand your impatience, but we can give you neither the perfect piece of advice nor exactly the consolation that would suit your case. All we can say is: Stick it out! Continue your studies and don't give up!

If you live to be eighty you've still got forty-one years of sex life ahead of you. *Frigid* means *cold*—and frigid women don't exist.

i. & s.h.

NB. See also Chapter 11 of this book, *Consumer Guide*.

Greedy For It Now

My husband has always travelled a great deal, and so I have found it natural to have sexual intercourse only once a week or once a fortnight. Not that I've ever got proper satisfaction out of it, because my husband (as I can see now) is a 'lousy lover'. It is only now that I have reached my forties that I have found my greed for sex being aroused.

At a dinner party I sat next to a man of over seventy. He was youthful, amusing and charming, and he was the life and soul of the party.

We had quite a lot to drink, and he offered to drive me home. On the way we agreed that I should go and see his home instead. After a few more drinks I found myself enjoying his caresses, which were cautious at first as it wasn't the sort of thing I was accustomed to. These led to more intimate caresses, and then kisses—you can imagine where.

Now I'm simply wild about him and visit him many times in the course of the week, and each time I have four or five or six perfect orgasms thanks to his eager, knowledgeable way of kissing.

He wants me to do the same thing for him.

What I want to ask you, seeing that sometimes I feel quite giddy afterwards, is this. Is it at all harmful to have so many orgasms at my age? And what about kissing him in the same way as he kisses me?

No, neither the one thing nor the other is harmful, but women are so easily distracted, so perhaps you ought to arrange a kind of division of labour? First you and then him?

It's so encouraging to hear about forty-year-olds who begin to find out new things—and about seventy-year-olds who are still going strong.

There's something so very positive about the fact that apparently even ladies in their forties can fall for 'But Miss Smith, I only wanted to show you my stamp collection'—and that they *like* falling for it.

Presumably the happiest solution would be if you could teach that globe-trotting wild tiger of a husband of yours a few of the lovely things you've just learnt? Surely *he* can't be too old either—or is he?

i. & s.h.

PS. We often reproach men for being apathetic and ignorant. But it is also up to a woman to show a bit of initiative.

'I've got two rooms plus an alcove. May I show you the alcove?'

Fantasies

I'm so unhappy. I've got the most wonderful husband in the world, and we get on wonderfully together—sexually as well as in other ways.

But .. and there is a 'but' . . . when I'm in bed with my husband, I never manage to have an orgasm if I just think about him. I have to think about various things, sometimes revolting things that I wouldn't dream of doing in reality.

One of my fantasies comes again and again. I try not to think about it, but when I notice my orgasm doesn't seem to be coming, I simply have to imagine this particular situation to myself. I imagine I'm bending over, and that a friend of my mother's has intercourse with me from behind, at the same time tickling me in front with his fingers. My mother is also present in some way or other, and takes part in it.

The whole thing is vague—it's them and yet it's not them. Their faces aren't very distinct, but I know perfectly well where this fantasy of mine comes from.

My father died when I was eleven, and then a man used to come and see my mother, and I dare say they used to make love together. One day I was standing in my room, naked, and bent down for something, when suddenly he was there in my room, and had his hand out and was tickling me while he unbuttoned his trousers and tried to press his penis into me. I remember being horrified and afraid, and that my mother came in and surprised us in the middle of it, and gave both of us a frightful telling off, and I cried and cried and never dared see him again.

I feel terribly perverted and have a horribly bad conscience about it as far as my husband is concerned. What can I do?

You can stop worrying about it. Most people, especially women, need fantasies of this kind to help fire their enthusiasm a bit. Especially women because they, as a rule, find it a little difficult to get into an erotic mood—and in particular find it harder to reach a climax. It takes them longer.

So fantasies of this kind—or some other kind—can help. We know a girl who likes to imagine she's being raped by four whopping great drunken Chinamen. She certainly wouldn't care to meet them in real life, but she needs them in this special situation, to whet her imagination.

Many men and women could tell you about their favourite

fantasies if they wanted to—but few would, because it's rather a private matter.

Some aren't afraid to tell the person they're married to about it, but sometimes the person in question isn't grown-up enough, or knowledgeable or tolerant enough, to be able to take it. Men in particular are terribly vain.

So it can definitely be both useful and necessary to give one's imagination free rein on certain occasions, but it may well also prove a little impractical. If you happen to be a female and are in full swing with a big, ruddy-complexioned baldpate of a monk who has started doing something dreadful but rather exciting, then you may find it a little distracting if your nice, grey-flannelled office-worker of a husband sticks his head in between and asks how you're getting on. Then you just get angry with the poor man, which is a pity, because he has no idea why and was taking such a lot of trouble!

In other words, take your whole family to bed with you in your imagination and use them without a bad conscience or any fear of being 'abnormal'.

We might as well explain a bit of the background to you. The situation, when you were eleven, was probably that you were approaching sexual maturity, and that you were somehow taken by surprise by this man. Perhaps you already suspected him of enjoying himself with your mother?

Well, he set something going in you that at once scared and attracted you. Consciously you only remember the scare, the shame, the horror and the fact that your mother scolded you— but somewhere down at the back of your mind is a memory of something strange, exciting, alluring and forbidden.

Most of us have had experiences similar to yours, and they often go to make up our particular sexual pattern.

Perhaps you will understand us a little better if we tell you two anecdotes from a study group we once had—two little stories that have got nothing to do with sex. One of the people taking part asked: 'Why is black pudding my pet abomination?' Well, we pried into his past a bit, and then he found the answer himself. 'Ah yes,' he said, and held out a hand on which one finger was missing. 'I was run over by a car when I was a boy. When I woke up in the hospital they'd lopped off one of my fingers. Shortly after they brought in my dinner . . . it was black pudding.'

'That's all very well,' said somebody else, 'but why don't I like milk?' We tried to delve into this, and finally it dawned on her. 'Ah, it must be because of my mother. No matter what was wrong with us, a headache or a sprained ankle, she always used to give us a big dose of castor oil which she "disguised" in a glass of milk.'

In conclusion we must say that it is seldom so easy to find the cause as it was in these two cases.

My Husband's Always so Keen!

I'm writing this because I've got an attack of bad conscience. My husband comes home from work at about half-past four and is always so keen and affectionate, and he can't understand why I'm not just as keen to go to bed and have a nice time with him. But I simply haven't got the energy.

And then I suddenly get nervous—is there something the matter with me? We have no children.

You'll soon have some if he keeps on like that. But joking apart, of course, you're not 'cold'. Frigid women don't exist! That's what we said recently—and you are no exception.

It so happens that men are more excitable than women—and as a rule their place of work is outside the home. Just imagine the howl that would go up if you appeared at his office and spread yourself across his desk! A housewife has to do the washing-up—or cook, or something else that happens to be her work, and naturally enough it keeps her busy. He'd better be a bit more ingenious and a bit more patient if he wants to get you away from the rissoles.

Attempts at improvization often fall flat in an organized relationship between two persons. But you should try to attune yourself to his afternoon whims—just once in a while. And he should take you out for dinner afterwards.

Enjoy yourselves!

i. & s.h.

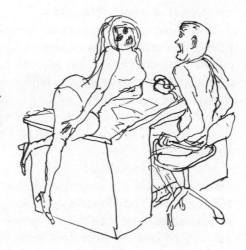

The home is a woman's place of work. Most men would be horrified if their wives came along to their offices and made demands on them.

My Husband Threatens to Leave Me!

We've been married for over fifteen years and have three children: a girl of fourteen and twins aged eight. We're very fortunate in every way except for the more intimate side of our lives. I'm not so keen on it as my husband, nor as often. I don't get much out of it.

I must admit he's been pretty patient with me, but recently it's as though he's got fed up with everything. He complains it's not very often I'm sweet and loving to him in this way, and he's told me about other women he knew when he was a young man, and that they were much more interested.

Several times recently he's threatened to leave me and the children, but by promising him it'll get better soon I've managed, so far, to persuade him to stay with us a little longer.

I'm scared stiff that he'll pack his bags and go—and I just don't know how I can make myself feel more like going to bed with him. I hope you can give me some good advice.

You're not the slightest bit *frigid*! Let us stamp out that superstition! Frigid women don't exist! *Frigid* means *cold*. And no woman is completely cold.

You raise a very important question in your letter. It's a problem which exists in masses of homes all over the world.

The husband claims that his wife is as cold as ice, as dull as ditchwater, uninterested, unwilling to cooperate, not keen, etc. What is the explanation?

The explanation lies in the fact that *most women are sexually cooler than most men*. Cooler—but not completely cold. Not frigid.

If you're a little less hungry than the other person, you can easily lose what little appetite you have if the other person hogs his (or her) food. Precisely the same thing applies to sexual relationships. The keen partner gets keener, and the not so keen partner becomes a little less keen than before and therefore *seems* uninterested in the eyes of the keener partner, but in point of fact is not uninterested.

That was a complicated explanation, but it's important for men as well as women to understand this. The majority of women are not as keen on sexual intercourse as their husbands. Of course there are men who are not so keen and women who are very keen, but such instances are much, much rarer.

The same applies in the animal kingdom. It is nearly always the eager male who chases after the less interested female.

You may think we're going back to Adam and Eve and piling it on endlessly, but this really is a problem we meet daily in our consultation. Every day there are men who complain that their wives show no interest in sex—and every day women come and ask: 'How can I become more interested?' Men complain and feel they've been so unlucky—and the women have bad consciences and think they're the only women in the world with this problem.

But this is the way things go in most homes! Can anything be done about it? Must we just accept it as a fact and say no more? *Can* women become more interested?

Yes, a great deal can be done. But first, both the man and the woman must realize where they stand: that they are both normal and healthy—that it is *normal* for a woman to be less interested —and that, together, they stand a good chance of getting much more out of their sex lives.

The man mustn't give up and think he's been 'unlucky'. The woman mustn't despair and think she's the only woman in the world who's 'cooler' than her husband. She's certainly not *cold* —just *cooler*.

Well, what can the man do then?

He must be patient, but not too reticent, because he is, of course, justified in taking pleasure and interest in this side of his relationship with his wife. It's his duty to study books on sex so that he can be a better lover—and he must talk to her about it.

What can the woman do?

She mustn't leave it all to her husband. It's her duty, just as much as his, to study the theory of sexual relationships. In the old days, a woman just wasn't supposed to have a sex-life at all. Today we know that it is more difficult for a woman to achieve a satisfying sex life than for a man, but this also means that she mustn't just lean back passively and wait for it to come toddling along by itself.

It's tough work—enjoyable, but undeniably tough work—to develop a good sexual relationship. It's certainly not something 'any damn fool can work out'. There are disappointments, problems, periods when things go worse—and periods when things go better—in any good sexual relationship.

So you must be prepared to talk to your husband about it, dear reader—even though it may be difficult for you in the beginning as you're not accustomed to doing so. You must accept his greater interest—just as he must accept your lesser. The interest increases with the pleasure.

'Appetite comes with eating' is what you hear sometimes. This applies even more to a woman's sex life: it comes slowly, but the interest is often aroused if the man is patient, gently insistent—and imaginative.

We wish you lots of happy love-making.

i. & s.h.

He Pesters Me!

I'm a young mother of nineteen and I've got two children aged one and two. My husband pesters me to sleep with him, but I'm afraid of having another baby, I just haven't got the time as I go out to work. My husband says it'll be all right, and of course I can use some kind of contraceptive, but you can't really trust any of them, can you? What I want to ask you because you're so good at answering questions, is do you think I should use a Dutch cap and then have intercourse?

We think we've got several good pieces of advice for you. It isn't always that we feel we can give good advice, so here's hoping you'll be able to follow it!

First, there's nothing in the world to stop you going to a doctor and getting him to give you a prescription for the Pill. It is a completely reliable method of contraception.

But we can read between the lines in your letter that something else is wrong too. You don't get any proper enjoyment out of going to bed with your husband. And the reason, quite simply, is that you and he don't know enough about it. It is true that even the most ignorant person in the world can manage to have children. But presumably man has been given his intelligence in order to make his life richer.

You and your husband must make both of your lives richer by *studying*, not just reading, some of the latest books on sexual relationships. You can borrow them from your local library.

The ideal thing would be to reach the point of never feeling 'pestered' when your husband suggests going to bed with you. But only very few women get this far.

For some reason or other a kind of loss of memory, or

amnesia, sets in where the pleasures of sexual intercourse are concerned—in women, that is. Most women forget, from one occasion to the next, that they too can get a lot of pleasure out of sexual intercourse (as long as the man is both knowledgeable and imaginative enough!).

i. & s.h.

When Men Were Men . . .?

I am forty-six years of age and have been married for almost twenty-five years. Our children are grown-up now and don't live at home any more, and it's as though I'm only just beginning to realize that something seems to be missing between my husband and myself. And if I try to look back, I feel it always has been missing. Perhaps not when we were very young. I don't quite know what to call it—the thing that's missing. Perhaps romance is the word that covers it best. When I read books and novels I find myself thinking there was much more romance in the old days. Nowadays everything is so technical and boring. In the old days things were somehow warmer, more sensitive. I don't think young people today are very romantic any more either. What can be the reason?

We feel many women think just the same way as you do. But this doesn't necessarily mean that you're right. We're all inclined to romanticize the old days, when Christmases were white and girls were girls. We forget that the lavatory was in the back yard, and that they never washed. We forget the diseases and the poverty and the uncertainty and the ignorance. And all the illegitimate children. 'Those were the good old days!' goes the song, but they were by no means *that* good. Ah well. Your marriage may still be a bit prosaic for all that.

It sounds as if you want to escape from the present, but it can't be done. Young people today—in their own way—are just as romantic as we were in our time. You'd better talk to your husband about it—and do something about it yourself. There's nothing like a few flowers, a bottle of wine, nice food, going off to see the old spots again, places where you and your husband can stroll along holding hands and saying 'Do you remember?'

Far too many wives leave everything to their husbands. All they're capable of is dissatisfaction and a kind of expectant attitude. Men are basically very thick-headed—they need to be spoon-fed, you know. Give him a nice big dose of sweet memories!

i. & s.h.

Am I Immoral?

I'm a young wife aged twenty-two. I've been married for three years and we've got two children and are a happy little family. My husband is kindness itself, and I hope I'll never lose him.

My question to you is on the subject of unfaithfulness. I myself don't think it's anything to get divorced for, but my husband says that if he found out I'd been unfaithful to him he'd ask for a divorce immediately, despite the fact that we love each other very deeply. He feels that when two people are married they virtually own each other, which I think is all wrong—crazy, in fact.

I myself have always been very liberal and found it difficult to say no, in other words I've been to bed with lots of men, and have no regrets about it whatsoever. Since I've been married, however, I haven't slept with anybody except my husband, even though I've felt like it.

But the other day it happened all the same. I did what I've been wanting to do for a long time—go to bed with somebody else. Don't judge me too harshly. I'm sure I'm not the only one who's done it, even though I love my husband.

The man I've been unfaithful to my husband with is my best friend's husband, which perhaps doesn't make things any better, but I haven't regretted it—on the contrary. But he and I have agreed that it had better be the first and last time, and that we'll keep it a secret, because we don't want to spoil things between the four of us.

Despite what has happened, nothing has changed between my husband and myself—if anything, perhaps, I love him even more than before. I've got a little secret now, something he doesn't know about, but I find that quite exciting.

If you print this letter I dare say many people will think my husband can't satisfy me in bed seeing I feel like sleeping with other men. But on the contrary, he's the only person who's ever given me an orgasm.

Well then, am I an immoral woman because I've been unfaithful to my husband? That's the question I hope you'll answer.

If you had been a man writing to us about having been unfaithful to his wife just on one little occasion, we believe that most people would have been fairly indulgent. Why heavens, most people would say, his wife ought to be proud of having such an attractive husband.

But a wife who is unfaithful to her husband—and doesn't even feel sorry about it! *Really!* Fancy making a cuckold of her poor fish of a husband like that! This is the official moral attitude; men are basically a lot of tough nuts and Don Juans, and their wives should be proud of having hooked them at all. But a wife who is unfaithful to her husband makes him look a poor sop. Such is the state of affairs today.

We protest at this. We say it's unfair, and you certainly don't 'own' the person you've married the way your husband claims.

We do not condemn you. We're admittedly a bit old-fashioned on this point and try to be 'true' to each other, but who can tell when one or the other partner may not be able to resist temptation? It's probably more important not to entertain the other person with accounts of your little lapses—or let them 'happen to slip out'.

We are possibly all on the way to adopting a more liberal attitude about this.

i. & s.h.

Wanton?

I'd like to ask you if you think I'm abnormal. We always read in your excellent column that it's men who want to have sexual intercourse and that women are never keen and are passive, etc. In our case it's the other way round. I'm twenty-two, have been married for two years and have a child aged three months.

It's not that my husband doesn't feel like sleeping with me, because he does, but I'm nearly always the one to take the initiative and start fondling him, and then I always think up so many little things which I feel ashamed of afterwards. I don't know what comes over me, but if we both enjoy it perhaps it's not wrong of me? Otherwise we get on wonderfully, my husband's lovely to be in bed with, and I have an orgasm every time, so really there shouldn't be any problems, but I just find myself wondering sometimes whether I'm normal? My husband says I'm not but at the same time he says he's never known any other woman to caress him like that, so I don't know, what am I to believe? I hope you'll answer this letter in your column.

Many men and many women will envy you, because you're

not the sort of person one meets *every* day. But you're certainly not abnormal. Isn't that nice to know?

We wish there were lots more like you.

i. & s.h.

Active Girl

You write so often that it's quite all right for a woman to take the initiative in making love. I've tried several times, but each time my husband has refused to have anything to do with me and made me feel ashamed and embarrassed. Now I don't dare any more, even though I believe that in his heart he'd like me to anyway. I'm forty-one.

You are the answer to many men's dreams and deserve to be praised! The fact that so many men can't face up to their dreams when they come true is not your fault.

You don't say which form or forms of sexual intercourse you use. If it's a form that is dependent upon his staying power, i.e. his erection, this may be the reason. Your husband is at the age (we assume you're both more or less the same age) when men can find it increasingly difficult to maintain an erection over a protracted period. Perhaps, at heart, he is embarrassed and nervous in case he should fail to keep it up. Talk to him about it. Be perfectly blunt and frank about it and try again.

Suggest the occasional thing that is not dependent on his penis but nonetheless gives you satisfaction. It should be easy for you to make this kind of proposal without hurting his feelings.

Have fun!

i. & s.h.

Bored

When I got to know my husband some four years ago, I had been to bed with a few men before, but had never had an orgasm during sexual intercourse with them.

They thought, like most men, that all that mattered was having a big, stiff thing.

Fortunately my husband was—and is—completely different. He immediately taught me to relax and enjoy everything he got up to. In the beginning I thought it was abnormal to use your mouth to kiss anything except somebody else's mouth, but nowadays it's only very seldom that I don't have an orgasm.

And we've got to the point where I, too, enjoy fondling and sucking my husband's penis, so from this point of view everything in the garden is rosy. In addition we're very fond of each other and get on fine in little everyday matters.

Well, by and large. Because there may be something slightly wrong with me after all. My husband has gone a little further in his wishes. He's told me he's also interested in girls wearing clothes made of rubber, leather, etc., and boots. Well, that's all okay, I just can't see any sexual connection, that's all. There's nothing I like more than looking smart in boots and a leather coat and so on, but it doesn't excite me sexually.

Well, we've chatted about it a good deal, and read about it here and there, including your column, and it's beginning to dawn on me that lots of people feel this way. And that's fine, I'm all for people helping each other to get as much out of their sex lives as possible.

He likes me to beat him too. And so on several occasions I've smacked him and whipped him and in a way I enjoy it when he comes—I mean, he obviously yearns for it. Even so, I feel so silly afterwards, because I can't understand him. I don't feel like hitting him. It doesn't make me excited. So for the next few days I always feel a bit out of gear.

Why can't I enjoy it, why don't I get excited seeing he loves it and loves me more than ever afterwards, while I just feel bored by it?

We've got on to the subject of men in women's clothes too, men who behave like maids to their wives. He's terribly keen on it, and sometimes I dig out a few bits of underwear and ask him to wash them for me. And give him a pair of panties and a slip to wear while he's doing it.

I've found out he likes it best if I talk to him like a sergeant-major, and of course it's easy enough, but I feel so silly.

I sometimes wish my husband had found himself a girl who really liked it, but he tried with various women when he was a bachelor, and it always went wrong.

It's not that he gets this way every time, but sometimes I can sense he feels it coming over him, and then he asks me to be a pal and really tan the life out of him, and he likes me to say when and how, so's he can look forward to it. But I have to go round trying to screw up my courage in the meantime.

First and foremost we think you have both achieved a great deal in the barely four years you've been married. Not many married couples have discovered so many things in such a short space of time.

We're sure you know the story about the native bearers who were made to hurry. Finally they refused to go another step, because they said, they had to wait until their souls caught up with their bodies.

You, dear lady, have been brought up to believe that men are big and tough, like John Wayne and Humphrey Bogart. Big silent men who smell of tweed and pipe tobacco and spend their time building bridges or being cowboys. *Proper* men.

And then you take a look at the man you managed to collar, and there he goes pottering round in nylon panties and a pink slip and says he wants to be smacked. Something's wrong!

Yes, something's wrong all right, but what?

It's actually our he-man ideal that is phoney, false and hypocritical. Your husband is an ordinary live human being with silly desires and notions just as everybody has in one way or another—and that includes you, and us.

John Wayne and Humphrey Bogart weren't he-men in reality either. Humphrey Bogart and his wives, for example, were always walloping each other, as all their friends knew. He wasn't the tough guy who just stood leaning up against a door with a cigarette dangling from his lips ready to take on all comers. He sat down and nursed a black eye with a hunk of raw

beef and ducked as ashtrays and rolling-pins came whining past his ears.

It's much easier for a man to be marvellous if you aren't married to him.

Your soul hasn't yet managed to catch up with all the things your husband has served up for you. It's hardly surprising. You simply haven't had time to dig out *your* little whims and wishes. You've been more or less smothered by having to agree to more than your emotions could take in.

Then there's the difference between male and female. Men are more easily excited, and a little faster and more directly, by clothes and thoughts and fantasies, whereas women are a bit slower to react. Sometimes your appetite only comes while you're chewing.

How about using a carpet-slipper on him to make him do the washing-up?

Few men grow to be older emotionally than eight or twelve

years at most. We've said this before, but that doesn't make it less true.

It takes time to build up confidence in each other—and in oneself. That's another old truism.

It'll all come in time.

i. & s.h.

Suppressed Bumpkin?

I got married young and soon had a couple of kids. I'm now thirty, and four years ago I got divorced from my husband.

Shortly after my divorce my doctor put me on to the Pill, with the result that I really started letting my hair down, and have got myself a good deal of experience in one way and another during the four years that have passed. (I'd like to assure 'respectable' readers that my sex life hasn't affected my children.)

Well, now I've met a man with whom I've fallen very much in love. The only trouble is I've had a hell of a time trying to stay faithful to him, because he never touches me. It doesn't matter if I tear off every stitch of clothing in front of him when he comes to spend the week-end with me. He still doesn't do a thing. I've tried caressing him, and he seems to like it. I've tried making him put his hand down between my legs, or on one of my breasts, but he just lets it rest there and doesn't do a thing.

When I've been fondling him for a bit here and there, he suddenly throws himself on top of me like some country bumpkin and bashes away. He holds my legs wide apart so I don't have a chance of moving them and joining in the fun.

It's driving me scatty, because I really am terribly fond of him. Now he says we ought to get married.

You'll probably say I ought to give him a piece of my mind, but surprisingly enough I'm terribly shy with him and just don't know what to say to him. He's been married before, and it's not as though he was impotent either, because he often has a rise without doing anything about it.

What's the matter? He says he's never loved anybody as much

*as he loves me and my children (who idolize him)—but does it mean
I just don't interest him as a woman?*

During the four years you have been gambolling around with
various men, you must have met types like him, men who don't
know much about women—and can't be bothered to find out
either. Well, that's putting things a little harshly, because it's
also partly the fault of the women, who feel shy and won't tell
them things.

You simply must talk things over seriously with him. It's the
major problem in far too many homes—people just don't dare
to talk about the most important things of all, things that affect
them both.

What's more, there's that sinister saying that problems that
exist before marriage don't get any less after.

i. & s.h.

Am I a Sex Maniac?

*My husband calls me a sex maniac because I nearly always feel
like going to bed with him. But isn't a sex maniac a person who
never experiences sexual satisfaction and is therefore insatiable?
I'm not insatiable and I get full satisfaction every time!*

You're worth your weight in gold. You're so right.

i. & s.h.

4. Men about women—and about themselves

In this and the previous chapter the problems are mainly—though not exclusively—those of mature couples. As a rule the letters come from people aged between twenty-eight and forty-five. The first waves of blind passion have subsided. One has sobered up a bit—and is slightly disappointed. The woman in the partnership has finally plucked up courage and said she doesn't get so very much out of it. Or else the man has got tired of trying and trying. The woman he ended up with wasn't a bit like those live-wire, grateful girls he used to know in his youth. His wife isn't a bit like the warm-blooded girl he fell for.

Wanted: A More Affectionate Wife

The problem I'd like to write to you about is what used to be known as 'frigidity' in women, whereas nowadays one talks about 'neglected' women. There's been a lot of talk about them in your column, and unfortunately I believe my own wife comes into this category. I say 'believe' because it's impossible to get her to talk about it. Sex isn't a subject we can talk about in our family. I've brought a few books on the subject home with me to see if it might help. She's read them, but never makes any comment. The cause of her passive attitude is undoubtedly to be found in the upbringing her parents gave her.

The problem is quite simply that my wife never dares to really 'let herself go' in bed. She's passive in the matter of caresses, which she's happy to receive but doesn't dare give. In fact she's very bashful in every way with me. I can't really find any reason for this. After all, she's thirty-six, and so really quite a big girl now. We have no other differences in our marriage in regard to other matters. But what can I do to solve my problem? I know she

*can be actively loving and affectionate, because it's happened once
or twice when her inhibitions were numbed by alcohol.*

Your letter could have been written by many, many men all
over the world. Women are a little less excitable, a little slower
to warm up than their husbands. This is a fact, but gently
persistent patience and tenderness can produce wonders.

On the other hand it is quite incredible how often married
couples find they can't talk to each other. Often it is the man
who refuses to discuss things, but also many women are much
too unresponsive when asked to discuss things frankly. You
mustn't give up hope, but it requires perseverance and, as we
say, patience on your part. What is involved is a difficult and
tedious process of de-upbringing, or re-upbringing, to counteract the one your wife was given in her home when she was a girl.

You've got many, many years of marriage ahead of you. You
must expect disappointments and some backsliding, but also
progress.

A bottle of good, cool champagne is an excellent and attentive
way of loosening inhibitions. The very fact that it's a rash sort
of thing to buy (on account of the price as well as in other
respects) may inspire your wife.

Even married women like to be wooed. This is something
married men often forget—or else they start wooing somebody
who is married to somebody else.

i. & s.h.

What About Garlic?

*I've been told garlic can make you more interested in sex. I need
some help, so I'd very much like to know if it's true and what's the
best way to eat it?*

Oysters, truffles, champagne, garlic and other spices have all
been credited in the course of time with the power to arouse
sexual desires.

They all work—provided you believe in them. But the smell of garlic is enough to make some people run a mile. You can also get garlic in capsule form at most chemists and it doesn't smell if you eat it in this way.

We would recommend pornographic photos. It's the most reliable and easiest method—at any rate for men. Women are a bit more complicated. But *reading* pornographic books often has an effect on women, whereas men can make do with looking at pictures.

i. & s.h.

Aphrodisiacs

Do you know of a really good aphrodisiac? Possibly a dinner for two?

We've heard of masses of things in the course of time. But most of them are doubtful.

For men, so-called pornography, i.e. pictures and/or books, is probably the most effective—a kind of mental aphrodisiac. If women are to see pornographic pictures they usually have to be of women. Naked women, half-naked women, several women together, women engaged in sexual play—but seldom naked men.

Ordinary films, with a spot of kissing and cuddling and what-not, and likewise romantic novels, would appear to stand a greater chance of having a sexually stimulating effect on women. As a rule, we must again add, because *what* and *how much* varies a great deal from one woman to another.

But everything seems to indicate that a little romance and a spot of wooing is the best way of leading up—something all too many married men forget.

Take your wife out so that she can escape from the washing-up, take her to a romantic film, a place where you can dance and have some dinner. Arrange things at home so that everything's peaceful—or go away for a week-end together. All this sort of thing is good and as a rule fruitful.

But let's go back to the suggestion for a romantic dinner *at home* as you asked us—even though a romantic dinner can be many different things.

It may be the meal a young woman prepares for the man she hopes to marry. It may be the way a wicked old wolf leads up to the seduction of his pretty, innocent secretary. We're not going to describe dinners of that sort.

Let us instead be extremely respectable and think of the kind of dinner a married man and a married woman—who, please note, are married to each other—might plan and enjoy in each other's company. It's possibly one of the most important kinds of romantic menu, a festive confirmation of the fact that you get on well with each other.

The children have been regaled with soda pop and cocktail sausages and are sleeping soundly. It's their parents' wedding anniversary, or some other day—or perhaps not any particular 'occasion' at all. Now they want to have a nice cosy time by themselves.

Aperitif

We start off with a Pernod. We both love this green, French absinth that tastes of liquorice-water. We also love rituals, so we've carefully brought proper absinth glasses home with us from Nice, and at Mougins, near Picasso's home, we bought a *doseur* to fix on the bottle. And as a finishing touch we've got semi-spherical bowls for ice-cubes which you place on top of the glasses so that the water can drip, ice-cold, down into the Pernod through a hole in the bottom. But of course all this isn't strictly necessary.

You can quite simply pour a measure of Pernod into a nice tumbler or beer-glass and add about a quarter of a pint of cold water with a lump of ice in it.

Hors d'oeuvre

Two (or four) big potatoes have been in the oven for an hour and are now ready. They've been slit, crosswise, on top and are then pressed open to make room for a big lump of butter. Wrap a small napkin round each. We finish our aperitifs. We each have a plate on which we have arranged some cool, fresh Iranian caviar, some finely chopped shallots and a quarter of a lemon. Then we use a big teaspoon to dig out the hot centre of the potato, swimming in butter—caviar, onion, a couple of drops of lemon and a little twist of the pepper-grinder—and the first mouthful slides down. We immediately feel thirsty. To celebrate the occasion we're going to have champagne, *half* a bottle of cool, dry Mercier. We don't know very much about champagne, but this firm received us warmly one cold, wet, grey December day at Epernay, near Rheims, and showed us round their champagne cellars in a Lilliputian train. We twist the cork out of the neck of the bottle carefully and pour out the first glass.

Main course

For our main course we're each going to have a small but very thick fillet steak. We've tied a slice of fresh lard round the edge, and we spice the steak itself at the last minute with thyme, salt and freshly-ground pepper. Then we give it a minute on each side—in piping hot butter and oil (half of each). Garlic butter, a few chips (or another baked potato) and a hunk of French bread—the right kind, an unsweetened *baguette*. We carry on with the champagne—and a little watercress, if we've been able to get some. (We don't eat the lard—or the string.)

Cheese

We follow up immediately with a bite of Emmentaler, or a blue cheese, with some more *baguette*, and finish off the champagne. We want to feel slightly elated, but have no wish to drink ourselves silly. We don't want to stuff ourselves with so much food that we can hardly move either—it would tend to spoil things.

Coffee

Now we come to our private little perversion. We like to serve coffee *before* the sweet. Just a small cup, together with a glass of Marie Brizard apricot brandy. (Not because we find it sexually stimulating, but because we feel coffee goes with *food*.)

Dessert

We might as well stick to apricots while we're at it, and so we serve a small portion of stewed, mashed apricots, sweetened with sugar and stirred together with whipped cream to make it ight and fluffy.

After which the really festive part can begin.

i. & s.h.

Wanted: Stiffness

I'm in my early forties. I'm in love with a girl (which is what I call her though she's my own age), but for certain reasons we can't be together as often as we would like.

To put things briefly, we're very fond of each other in bed too, and if I can't satisfy her in the 'normal' way, well, I've got two hands and a mouth. But I don't think my penis gets sufficiently stiff, even though I get an erection of sorts. Sometimes, at all events, it's difficult to get it in, and it's a bit of a shame if she has to stand on her head . . .

I've spoken to a doctor about it a long time ago. He gave me some injections, but he wouldn't tell me what the stuff was called, and I rather suspect it was just ordinary vitamin C. I think this doctor may have quietly thought to himself I was talking nonsense. Well, the long and the short of it is this, would you be so kind as to tell me the name of the correct medical preparation that may be able to help in such cases? I fully realize you're not allowed to boost any particular pharmaceutical firm, but surely there must be various preparations on the market?

I'd like to mention that I'm not a mental wreck, nor has my self-esteem suffered a 'cruel blow'. But damn it all, I'd like to be able to make her completely happy if possible. The fact that she seems to be perfectly contented with the present variation is another matter.

It is really a question of mental attitude. Many people will claim that this, that or the other thing has helped. But faith moves mountains, so presumably faith can also . . .

In other words, the day you're not interested in having a better erection in order to please your girl-friend, you'll have a better erection.

Do you understand what we mean? Uncertainty, self-sacrifice, showing consideration, fear of a fiasco, etc. make you slightly impotent in the old-fashioned sense of the word. The day you realize she means what you yourself write, namely that she is perfectly happy and satisfied with the way things are now, your problem will disappear.

You are potent.

PS. But see also the Consumer Guide at the end of this book.

And So Forth

I'm married to the sweetest and most understanding wife in the world. We get on famously and both have the most wonderful orgasms, so that's not the problem.

So far I've controlled myself, but I feel a fantastically strong urge to have a go with several women at once—well, one other besides my wife. When we go to parties I find myself itching to pinch strange women's bottoms and so forth.

My wife and I have discussed it openly and she has given me permission to try this noble sport, but she doesn't wish to join in. I only want to if she wants to as well. How can I get rid of these unnatural thoughts?

Bury yourself in gastronomy, as I have done. But it makes you fat.

I fully understand your desire for variation and sweetbreads in *sauce suprême*. Creamed morels are simply delicious, too.

And what do you say to Russian *blinis* with caviar, a touch of finely chopped onion and a little *smetana*?

Many of the so-called pornographic films that can be hired or bought nowadays feature one man and two girls. Wouldn't this take the edge off your appetite?

You have an unusually sweet and understanding wife, and perhaps your problem is that everything is going so well you feel like doing a bit more experimenting.

I know all these reflections don't solve your problem, but I'm afraid I've got nothing better to offer. Sorry.

s.h.

What Every Man Should Know

For thirteen years I've been an egoistic oaf towards my wife. But not on purpose.

About six months ago I woke up with a bang. My wife told me she'd been to bed with two men (one at a time) just to find out whether it was her or me there was something the matter with.

And she said now she knew it wasn't her.

This was quite a nasty smack in the eye, but it helped. We had a number of plain talks and discussed a lot of things. We read your book and a couple more—and I learnt a great deal.

So then we got started again, and admittedly to begin with she felt downright revulsion at fondling me and my genitals. But we're getting there.

But the worst of it is she still only feels like sleeping with me about once a month. In the intervening period she's completely dead. She's by no means dissatisfied with me any more. She claims I'm better than any other man she's known—and I've certainly never seen her get into such a state of ecstasy before. She's practically unconscious by the time we've finished.

And she says herself she couldn't wish for a better husband. She admits that she probably has a basic need for sexual intercourse more often, but that she just can't bring herself to it—can't get sexually excited any more frequently.

You've been taught a lesson of the kind many men are taught. The lucky ones. Other men are not so lucky and just bash ahead stupidly convinced of their own excellence.

Let's agree, man to man, that we can never hope to be as exciting to our sorely tried wives as another man, a complete stranger. That's why we must make a greater effort than the men our wives come into contact with by chance. We cannot wholly compensate the admiration they arouse in our wives, but we can try.

We must also remember that women are stimulated indirectly far more than men. It's not photographs and sexy words and thoughts that arouse a woman's desires, but soft words and sweet music and other forms of romanticism. Go out and eat, dance, go to the cinema.

You must quite simply try to pretend that your wife is a girl you've never seen before but whose heart you're setting out to win—by means of letters, flowers, little gifts and consideration and kind thoughts and lots of other things.

You forget it, and I forget it, and all married men forget it. It ought to be tattooed on the backs of our hands—on the back of our left hand so that we'd see it every time we looked at our watches.

And it shouldn't just apply to critical situations, but for the rest of our married lives. It's far more important than brushing our teeth, filling up the car with petrol, and that daily apple that's supposed to chase the doctor away.

It's a very important part of the struggle involved in keeping a marriage going. And it's the greatest fun.

s.h.

PS. Women in general are not so fascinated by men's John Thomases as men themselves are. Some women learn to be a bit more fascinated in time, but it depends on the men.

Sex Before and After Birth

A year ago my wife had a baby and it was a little difficult to get into the swing of things after the birth. But it was all right, and I got what I wanted.

My wife would often get into a state of ecstasy and sound as if she was enjoying it. But a couple of nights ago, when she thought I was asleep—we'd just had sexual intercourse—she started to masturbate.

I pretend not to notice until I heard her groaning and go completely rigid. Then I gave her a good spanking, and afterwards she told me, sobbing, that for the last year or so she'd never had an orgasm.

I was shocked to find that a woman could put on such an act. Now she's moved into the boy's room and won't have anything to do with me after that walloping.

She's cut out all your columns, and asked me to read them. I've learnt a lot, but she still won't allow me to show her what I've learnt.

What does a foolish, ignorant man like me do now?

Please excuse my handwriting. I am nervous and ashamed.

Actually it's your wife who's been neglected, and we fully understand her spitefulness. You ought to show her this.

You spanked her because she didn't get anything out of sleeping with you—and because she pretended to be delighted in order to please you and satisfy your male vanity. You've behaved like an awful boor, and you should ask her to try to forgive you.

In their report on the sexual habits of human beings, Masters and Johnson say that women as a rule become rather disinterested in sex during the first three months, but that during the middle three months of their pregnancy are often more interested than when they are not pregnant!

Furthermore, Masters and Johnson state that it seems as if women who breast-feed their children get back into the swing of sexual intercourse a little faster than women who do not breast-feed their children.

It looks as though the sucking of the nipple sets a hormone into motion which, amongst other things, causes contractions of the womb and is perhaps at the same time sexually stimulating.

But then your wife was interested in sex too. It was you who failed to follow up this interest.

i. & s.h.

Whoops—It's All Over!

I think I need to be told the merciful truth—a sort of coup de grâce.

I've got to the state where I can't last longer than thirty to sixty seconds before I ejaculate. It isn't a very long time if the woman is supposed to get something out of it as well.

I dare say I've been hoping somewhere at the back of my mind that my wife was frigid—then things would balance a bit better. But it seems she's perfectly capable of having an orgasm—just not with me!

I've been to see several psychiatrists, but all they say is: 'Think of something else!' That advice just doesn't work! I'm a neurotic with an Oedipus complex, scared stiff of that marvellous, terrifying creature called woman. I just can't live up to her expectations. Whizz, bang—ejaculation. Impotent.

Women are difficult—but what would we do without them?

Should I face up to facts, continue to live my more or less cock-eyed sex life or stick to masturbation and peeping?

I'm thirty-nine.

You should stop showing off. Oedipus complex, neurotic, etc. Come off it! It's simply a matter of your not knowing enough about how a man can satisfy a woman sexually without using his penis.

And then you experience the same thing as most men, namely that your ejaculation comes too quickly. This makes you nervous, and the next time the same thing happens again—a vicious circle which most of us get into at some time or another.

Read a few of the latest books on sexual techniques and then see that with the help of a finger, a tongue, an electrical vibrator or in some other way, you should get your lady well and truly warmed up, then see to it that she has an orgasm—and then, but not until then, should you let your penis come into the picture. Then you will discover that your problem (and your wife's) has been solved.

But it can't be done from one night to the next. The subject has to be studied and thoroughly discussed, and you will have to experiment a bit until you and she find the right method.

Good luck!

i. & s.h.

PS. You can also train yourself. See the Consumer Guide at the end of this book.

Impotent?

I'm in my mid-thirties—that's all. But I'm already suffering from what I suppose you call premature impotence.

It started some sixteen years ago when I tried to have sexual intercourse with a girl. But I found I was impotent—couldn't get a proper erection. It was a very unpleasant experience, and things haven't improved since. My doctor said he felt my impotence was the symptom of a neurotic disorder.

The problem naturally still worries me a great deal. I wonder if you can give me any advice?

We understand your impatience and we can help you. But in order to do so you will have to follow carefully, using your intelligence as well as your feelings, the line of thought we will now sketch for you.

You started a relationship with a woman but got off to a bad start. The result is a vicious circle which needs breaking.

Furthermore you are under the delusion, like so many men, that potency has something to do with being able to bounce up and down on top of a girl for hours on end—with an erect penis.

If only you realized how many girls have groaned with irritation underneath ignorant sexual athletes who, like yourself, have misunderstood the term *potency*. To be *potent* has nothing to do with endurance. Nor has it anything to do with erection. *Potency* and *potent* mean *ability* and *able*. To be potent means capable of satisfying your partner in a sexual relationship. (And we'd even moderate it a little and say: being in a position to offer your partner a means of obtaining sexual satisfaction—because it shouldn't constitute any form of pressure on the other person).

But to get back to the point: it is very, very seldom that a woman derives any sexual satisfaction from a man who just bashes away unimaginatively.

We've mentioned this before, but no doubt we'll have to go on saying it a great many times: the little button that switches on a woman's sensation of erotic pleasure is placed in such a way that very few women experience sufficient titillation during ordinary sexual intercourse. This little button, known as the clitoris, is situated just above the entrance to a woman's vagina. It's a very sensitive organ with masses of nerves in it.

A woman's vagina is not particularly sensitive. For thousands of years, however, men have judged by themselves and assumed that since they thought it felt so wonderful to be inside a woman's vagina, women must find it equally marvellous. It's not as simple as that.

Most women find it necessary to have their clitoris tickled in a special way, with a finger, a tongue or something else. We have had many letters from people who have recommended an electric vibrator as being a wonderful help. (See the Consumer Guide at the end of this book.)

But most men get stuffy and offended because they think it is a disavowal of their potency. (It is accepted that women are vain. It is probably true that women are vainer than men on certain points. But when it comes to potency, men's vanity is enormous.

It has prevented masses of married couples from working out forms of sexual intercourse that can lead to the sound and pleasurable development of their relationship. Vanity and ignorance combined, that is.)

And now we're getting near the answer.

Forget all that nonsense about potency in the old-fashioned sense of the term. Realize, quite clearly, that any man can give any woman sexual satisfaction without being a sexual athlete. That he can do so merely with the help of a spot of imagination, inventiveness, tolerance and a few other things up the same street and, on the part of a woman, a spot of willingness, not too much prudishness, and a slight desire to experiment.

When you have grasped this and got to the point where you can give your lady the most delightful forms of sexual satisfaction without using your penis, you can then, when she is content, use your penis for your own pleasure. You will discover that when you no longer feel any obligation to get an erection just to please the lady, the problem will have completely disappeared.

i. & s.h.

Is She Simulating?

How can a man work out whether a woman really has had an orgasm? Or whether she's just pretending because she feels she's being difficult, or abnormal, or is afraid I may leave her.

What are the typical signs that a woman has had an orgasm? And how can you detect if she's putting on an act?

A man can't. By far the majority of women can put on this act very convincingly—and most of them either have done it or still do it.

You get a straight answer only when the woman feels so confident that she's not afraid to speak her mind openly.

i. & s.h.

She Screams

*What shall I do? My fiancée, a lovely girl, screams at the top
of her voice when she has an orgasm.*
It's very impractical.

Some of our friends had precisely the same problem, and one
day the neighbours called the police, who rang the door-bell
and asked: 'Is anybody being murdered here?' Our friend
answered: 'On the contrary!'

Things are a bit easier when you're married and have a home
of your own, but properly speaking it's the sort of situation that
requires, ideally, a completely detached and sound-proof house.

Of course she can control herself and keep her screams back,
but it spoils things a bit. It would be better if your fiancée could
somehow transfer her emotional outburst to something else,
like heaving at a rope, or bursting a bag of cornflakes, or some
other method by which she could express her passions in a
quieter way.

You'll have to devise something!

i. & s.h.

Not With His Wife

*I've just married, for the umpteenth time, a lovely young girl.
Before we got married there was nothing the matter with my desire
to go to bed with her, but since our wedding I just don't feel like
having sexual intercourse with her at all. But I find I'm capable of
making love to several other girls in the course of a single evening.*

*The same phenomenon has manifested itself every time I've got
married.*

What shall I do? It upsets me badly.

I don't think we can solve your problem by letter.

It sounds completely crazy. We can only suggest a couple of
possibilities.

Could it be that these chance female acquaintances don't make any demands on you? We're thinking, for example, that you may find it cramps your style if you keep thinking that you're supposed to be helping your wife to have an orgasm.

Chance female acquaintances, especially if you pay for their favours, don't make the same demands. Furthermore, chance female acquaintances are as a rule warmer and keener because women also find a completely different man more exciting.

Or could it be that in your heart you nurse an unfortunate, romantic notion that the girl you love and are married to is—too pure for sex?

We're inclined to believe that psychoanalysis, or some other form of psychotherapy, will be needed to clarify matters.

i. & s.h.

Are Doctors Allowed To?

Some time ago my wife and I decided to have her pregnancy terminated for social and health reasons and therefore made an official application for an abortion.

My wife is quite young and rather shy, and so it was most embarrassing for her to be asked how often we had sexual intercourse, when, and in which way, and whether she had an orgasm every time or not.

Naturally she didn't dare refuse to answer in case her application should be refused, but I can't help wondering whether questions of this kind are necessary. Or could they be mainly for the perverted enjoyment of lascivious doctors?

It may seem a bit peculiar to you that your wife should have had such detailed questions put to her. A number of them, we feel, should not be strictly necessary in order to decide the question of abortion. You may be right in thinking that your situation was, to a certain extent, unfairly exploited.

The end justifies the means, they say. We feel it is hardly likely that the doctor will have posed these questions for personal, lascivious reasons. The point is that we still have far too little scientifically collated knowledge of what takes place between two people. This is because we have a taboo on sex—still.

The doctor in question has thus tried to get to know a little more about something he was given no chance of studying at college. Don't you feel we could give him this break? Then there's a chance of his passing it on to his colleagues—who have also had to work hard to find out what little they know—by going round the authorities.

The result would be that doctors would be in a better position to advise their patients than hitherto. Surely this is a worthwhile aim?

i. & s.h.

Something Important About Development

My wife and I are beginning to work out our sex lives. I think. We're twenty-eight and thirty-one, and after many difficulties and disappointments I think things are going pretty well.

The problem is that my wife is dissatisfied. It's very hard to get her to join in the fun each time. She says it costs her an awful effort to get as far as an orgasm—so she's rather pessimistic.

Just at the moment things are pretty awful. We've just had a couple of fiascos.

There are several factors involved.

First, women, as we've mentioned before, really do have a harder time getting anything out of their sex lives. In other words it is actually *harder work* for a woman.

Secondly, some peculiar mechanism seems to exist which actually gives women a loss of memory in connection with their sex lives. A lovely orgasm, a really nice, successful time in bed is often forgotten by a woman when the time comes round to try again. But she'll remember the disappointments and the defeats all right. Rather impractical, but that's how it is.

Lastly, there's a rule which says all forms of development take place by leaps and bounds. You'd expect things to get steadily better. Just a little bit better every time. But no form of development takes place like that. Not even growth in height or weight takes place regularly, unnoticeably. Anybody who can remember the time he (or she) took driving lessons will recall that the actual process of learning was a bit jerky too. After a few unsatisfactory lessons during which you thought you drove appallingly, there suddenly comes a lesson in which everything seems to go marvellously.

The same applies to sexual relationships. Things go well for a couple of times, then sort of middling, then marvellously, then not so very well, then a bit better again, and so on. Menstruation or a birth or time spent away from home can turn the clock back, so to speak, and you feel you'll have to start all over again. It's very important to know this. Even people who know it all perfectly well often find themselves forgetting it.

Over every marital bed there should, be a notice in fiery characters reading: *All development takes place by leaps and bounds*. Successes are followed by fiascos, and then you make progress again.

i. & s.h.

Giddy-up, Little Girl!

I'm thirty-five and my wife is twenty-eight. We've been married for six years and as yet have no children. My wife's lovely, but we've never got anything out of sex. I have a very loving nature, but my wife is more or less the opposite. We've often discussed it, and have bought and read various books, but nothing has done any good.

About six months ago I said to my wife: 'What can we do to make things better?'

She replied: 'Buy a riding-whip and use it!'

I was terribly shocked. I told her she ought to go and see a doctor, but she refuses to do so, and since then there's been no sex between us. My wife continues to run the house and do her work as if nothing had happened, but I don't feel too good.

What an awkward situation! On the one hand you're lucky enough to have an honest wife who isn't afraid of stating her problem. On the other hand it's unfortunate that you should be shocked, unhappy and unsympathetic.

In a way we understand you well. But we also know that there are many people who feel the way your wife does. We've got piles of letters—we could fill this whole column with them—from people with a similar outlook. So it's by no means entirely unusual. But it was something very new to you, and came as a shock.

We understand your wife, too. And it's not the sort of thing a doctor can deal with. Protracted, arduous and costly psychiatric or psychological treatment could reduce the problem a little, but hardly remove it altogether.

The best thing would be if you and your wife could come to some sort of compromise. This suggestion will probably shock both you and others, but then people's minds often work in a more kinky fashion than you'd think. It's more realistic to try to live with this knowledge than just to be horrified and try to thrust the problems away from you, under the surface. You can press a rubber ball down under the surface of the water too, but it requires a constant expenditure of energy—and this creates tensions.

i. & s.h.

PS. We'd like to praise your wife once more for having found words to express her desires. It's rather a shame for her that you should have reacted so violently and negatively. It doesn't promote confidence between man and wife. But this sort of thing is seldom talked about, so your reaction is understandable, though, as we say, unfortunate.

Would it help you if we mentioned that masses of men would be glad to help your wife?

Please have a look at the chapter entitled *Special Problems*.

Only One in a Hundred?

Is it natural, perverted or immoral to kiss a woman's clitoris with your tongue in the course of love-making? And for her to do the same thing to the man's genital organs?

It's very titillating and arouses strong feelings. I think it's a beautiful and natural thing between two people who love each other. What do you think?

Is it a very rare thing, or is it normal for people to arouse each other's sexual excitement in this way? (Some say you'll only find one person out of a hundred doing it. Is that true?)

It's normal and common. Kinsey, in his report on the sexual behaviour of white Americans, mentions that it increases proportionately with education, i.e. that it is more widespread among people who have attended school for many years than among people who left school at an early age.

(But there's no need to conclude from this that it's something Americans learn at school.)

i. & s.h.

Miserable

I got married five years ago to a beautiful girl of nineteen. I was twenty-three at the time. Before and just after our marriage we had a wonderful time, although my wife never had an orgasm.

We talked it over, but she couldn't properly explain in what way I should make a bigger effort and so forth. I asked her to ask a doctor, but that didn't help. During the last few years—it seems a long time—things have been going very much downhill sexually speaking as I've noticed more and more that my wife does it more or less to please me. On top of it all, hard work and financial troubles. It's all made me very nervous and we live together without sex. I've been unfaithful to my wife a couple of times, otherwise I've learnt to look after myself.

We wouldn't dream of leaving each other. I couldn't live without my wife.

The way things are now we just can't talk to each other about it any more. We can hardly face looking at each other in the mornings.

The majority of us manage to find out how to have children.

Men and women work this sort of thing out—and women don't have to experience any sort of feelings at all. It's not until we permit ourselves the luxury of demanding that a woman should get something out of her sexual relationships as well that the difficulties begin.

It's actually like learning to play the violin. You can't just start scraping away at the strings. It takes time and practice and a bit of an ear for music and imagination—but not more than most of us can manage.

Let's go back to your remark 'We had a wonderful time, although my wife never had an orgasm.'

That's what you wrote. Now just imagine going to a restaurant and sitting down at the same table, day after day. You're hungry and in fine form and you study the menu and give the waiter your order. Half an hour later they tell you the kitchen has closed. Day after day you try, and each time you get fooled.

That's how your wife has felt for a long time! So you mustn't expect her to believe, all of a sudden, that now the kitchen is open and ready to serve her.

i. & s.h.

PS. Please see Chapter 11, *Consumer Guide.*

Never Comes

I'm forty-five and when I go to bed with my girl I have a difficult time coming. It isn't as if I wasn't keen and there's nothing wrong with my erection. What would you advise?

Sorry! We've got nothing to advise in your case. We can do little more than point out that it may be a question of boredom. Maybe you dream about something or other you'd rather fancy but which you daren't propose. Or which you know your girl will refuse?

Maybe that's not your problem. It would probably reveal itself as lack of interest on your part anyway. It's a problem in many marriages. Neither men nor women are as monogamous as our marital system demands.

So it's nice if you can be a bit understanding towards one another, and thus avoid things ending in unfaithfulness.

We remember a play that was on some time ago. It was about a couple who amused themselves by dressing up for each other. She hired a Girl Guide uniform, and he dressed up in black shiny shorts and boxing gloves. Or else she would be a nurse and he was just a patient whom she bossed around. Or else she'd put on a wedding dress, complete with veil and orange-blossom, and he'd doll himself up like a speedway motorcyclist complete with crash-helmet, etc.

No doubt it will sound crazy to most people the first time they hear it. But on second thoughts it must be admitted that it's an amusing and imaginative way of livening up your marriage. We've been thinking about it, and we think it's a lovely way of sorting out the deadlock which wedlock often becomes.

i. & s.h.

Where Does It Come?

I read somewhere that a man's orgasm is supposed to come, or is felt, in the head of the penis, the glans, and that it is a fundamental error to believe that it comes in the prostate.

So then I began to wonder if there could be something the matter with me. I thought a prostate orgasm was the right kind? In all humility, and with great caution, I've asked various colleagues, both old and young, and by and large they all believed they felt their orgasms somewhere up in their abdomens. They are all men.

'It's as if you were having a marvellous, warm nail drawn through the rear part of your urethra,' said one of them.

But now comes the strange part. When I produced this quotation from the book that claims the right kind of orgasm takes place up in the head of the penis, they all began to admit that it had happened to them too, a quite incredible, wonderful experience, but very rare.

So my question to you is, how does one go about it? Is it something that can be learnt?

Your question takes us completely by surprise. It's never been a problem for any of us, but it's become one now.

We can't answer your question, but we can appeal to our male readers. Does anybody know anything about it?

We were just beginning to extricate ourselves from the absurd discussion about vaginal orgasms as opposed to clitoral orgasms in women. We men have had an easy time of it for too long. Now maybe it's our turn.

s.h.

How Often?

We've been discussing what sort of difference exists between the number of times a man and a woman can have an orgasm within a given period of time.

The whole thing started when somebody claimed that prostitutes who behave as if they're having orgasms in point of fact always simulate—and I was inclined to agree with him.

The same person, however, claimed that a man would be capable of having the same number of orgasms as a woman within a period of, say, twelve hours.

I don't think so.

Prostitutes don't have orgasms with their customers. Of course a prostitute may have a customer for whom she develops special sympathy—or who takes particular trouble to find out something that really gives her pleasure. But it's very seldom. And somehow it's not the point of going to a prostitute either. But a lot of men are so romanticized they happily imagine the girl has chosen them because of their particular charm—and then they embroider on this story. Often the true facts of the matter would be so brutal for them to hear that the pleasure would be destroyed.

A good number of wives would be in a position to state that their husbands had been capable of having about two thousand orgasms during the past twenty years—without their ever having had a single one. But we don't suppose you're thinking of people of this kind.

If we take an average man and an average woman, both of whom are capable of having orgasms during sexual intercourse, the woman is capable of having more orgasms than the man.

Kinsey's assistant, Pomeroy, tells of a sixty-year-old woman who was capable of having fifty orgasms in twenty minutes. She'd never had an orgasm until she was past forty. She is undoubtedly an exceptional case, but nobody has ever heard of a man being capable of having so many orgasms—not in the course of twelve hours either. Two or three times in the course of twenty-four hours would make most men feel really proud, whereas skilful women can attain a much higher score.

Don't let's give more ordinary souls inferiority complexes. One can easily manage on less.

i. & s.h.

In the Bus

I'm a bachelor aged forty-four. Every morning I have a terrible time. I have an erection, even when I travel to work, and I find it most embarrassing. I have to hold my briefcase in front of me in the bus. Do you know an effective means of keeping it down?

Yes, women!

That's a rather facile answer, but obviously if you get rid of the sperm and the sexual desires that accumulate at intervals, then the problem is solved. You seldom read cookery books after a big dinner, if you understand what we mean.

Masturbation is also an excellent way of appeasing acute hunger. We often use the simile—while we're on the subject of eating—that just as a portion of fish and chips can be an excellent way of appeasing your appetite, masturbation is a fine thing too. Naturally most people prefer a cosy little dinner in the company of somebody they're fond of. A spot of well-cooked food, a nice bottle of wine, plenty of time and pleasant surroundings—but if the desire is acute and you simply can't take your mind off it, then some fish and chips from a local stall is an excellent way of appeasing that desire.

But it's not always we can find the time and the opportunity to indulge in those cosy little satisfying dinners.

i. & s.h.

How Can I Become a Sexual Acrobat?

I'm a young man of nineteen and I'm going steady with a lovely girl of sixteen.

Is it natural that I can only manage it once—and that I've finished after three or four minutes?

I would so like to be able to keep going a bit longer. I haven't tried so very much. When I've had a bit to drink, just five beers, for instance, I can keep it up much longer. But still only once.

Yes, it's very common at your age to come more quickly than one would like. It's also common for beer to have a delaying effect and make ejaculation a bit more difficult—when consumed in such large quantities, that is.

You write: 'just five beers'. That's quite a lot, you know. (Small quantities, a bottle of strong beer, a couple of whiskies or a quarter of a bottle of wine, however, can be just right for women who need to loosen some of their tiresome inhibitions.)

But you're on to quite the wrong train of thought—like most other men who don't know so very much about women—and just like most women who don't know so very much about themselves.

There's an old superstition that women love sexual athletes who can hammer away for hours on end. But it applies only to women who don't know any better. We've touched on the question before, and it would take up too much space to repeat it. We can only advise you to go to the library and get hold of some of the latest books on sexual enlightenment and study them carefully.

Men who think everything rests on physical prowess are hopelessly naïve and really are 'lousy lovers'.

PS. If—for one reason or another—you wish to delay the moment of your ejaculation, it is a matter of training.

It can be done in this way. Both partners concentrate on titillating the man just to the point of orgasm. A man can feel very clearly when he's just about to come. When he does so, he makes a sign, and they both stop. In a little while they carry on again. And then stop again, and then continue. Now and again something'll go wrong and he'll ejaculate anyway, but gradually he'll get better and better at telling his partner when to stop, thus avoiding ejaculation.

This form of training can then be continued inside the woman's vagina. Again, it'll go wrong a few times, but gradually get better and better.

Then comes the final phase, namely when he finds himself able to wait for her when her orgasm is about to come, so that they can achieve simultaneous orgasm. Of course when he notices her excitement mounting, this in itself will excite him and make it more difficult to hold back his ejaculation. But this, too, is a matter of training.

                                                                i. & s.h.

5. Masturbation

Masturbation in marriage, masturbation amongst young people, and masturbation as practised by unmarried individuals— unfortunately it's all still a very big problem. Unfortunately, because masturbation in marriage, amongst children and young people and unmarried individuals, is a completely natural thing that shouldn't give rise to any form of mental torment. Two people can also masturbate together—whether they do it to themselves or to each other. All perfectly in order.

Masturbation is healthy, masturbation is instructive, masturbation relieves the tensions and helps you to relax—and it's lovely.

It worries a lot of people. Is it harmful? Can one overdo it? Do you risk becoming deformed? All utterly unfounded fears.

Much of it can be traced back to the monstrous misinterpretation of the Book of Genesis, Chapter 38, verses 4 to 10, in which Onan goes to bed with his deceased brother's wife but doesn't want her to become pregnant. He therefore practises *coitus interruptus*, i.e. withdraws just before ejaculating and lets his seed fall on the ground instead of depositing it inside his sister-in-law's vagina. According to the strict Levite laws it was his duty to help his deceased brother to have some children. His brother had died childless, and Moses had ordered them to produce children. Onan merely 'took his pleasure'.

This story has been completely misunderstood and given rise to the terms onanism and masturbation. And this is how our pleasure has been destroyed.

Rubber Member

I would like to ask you to be so kind as to help me, if possible, by telling me where I can buy two different forms of rubber penis.

1. One of them is the kind that enables two women to have sexual intercourse with each other at the same time, i.e. long and smooth.

2. The other is for individual use, i.e. something I can use to masturbate with. I once saw one in a nudie magazine that could tickle you because it had a sort of attachment to bring on an orgasm more quickly and easily.

Any address, even abroad, would be welcome.

We seem to remember having seen examples of the first kind in *Love's Picture-book* edited by Brusendorff and Henningsen, but have no idea where they can be bought. Perhaps our readers can help?

The other kind can be bought at various small shops, but we haven't seen any with special 'ticklers' on. We should be very interested to have further information from our readers.

i. & s.h.

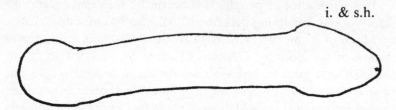

Solidly made rubber penis with a hole in the right-hand end and a bulb at the left-hand end so that it can be made to squirt. We're not allowed to say *where* these dummy penes are available because their sale is forbidden without a prescription! (See also our *Consumer Guide*.)

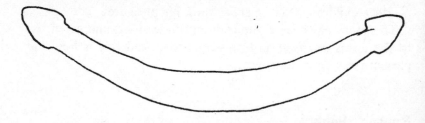

Double penis made of rubber.
Designed for ladies who are more or less in agreement.

PS. Shops we have asked have promised to try to get hold of No. 1. We've also found a delightful Japanese foam rubber penis substitute in white (see the illustration, which is life-size).

PPS. Stop press! Both the 'push-me-pull-you' and the one with the tickler now found!

Japanese rubber penis of white foam—decorated. Life size. Smart without being ostentatious.

Out of Shape?

I've masturbated ever since I can remember. My problem is that it's made my penis go out of shape.

I'm terribly ashamed of this and daren't go anywhere near girls. Just supposing I went to bed with a girl and she found out I wasn't normal just in the very place where she'd expect me to be!

Do you think an operation would put me right again? I'm fifteen.

Please forgive the jokey heading, but we took the liberty because it just isn't a problem at all. At least it *shouldn't* be a problem.

All men are 'out of shape' just there. So it's completely normal. Few men incline to the right. Most incline to the left.

You may say you haven't noticed this much in men's changing rooms and the like, but this is because it is most clearly seen when the penis is filled with blood, i.e. erect. But tailors know it and cut trousers accordingly.

A great many young people have the most dreadful problems in connection with the appearance of their genital organs. This applies in particular to girls and women, who after all have little opportunity to see what other women's genitals look like.

One of the good things about all the pornographic booklets full of pictures that have appeared in recent years is precisely the fact that there are so many close-ups of women's sexual organs. You can't always count on those of the men, for they've usually been picked for size.

i. & s.h.

Masturbation

You've written so much about masturbation being harmless. Well, to a certain extent I believe you're right, but not long ago I read in Love Without Fear *that if the larger vaginal lips aren't able to cover the smaller ones it may be due to masturbation. That's just my problem, my outer vaginal lips are too thick.*

I've masturbated a lot, ever since I was a little girl, but as far as I can tell from snapshots of myself as a child I used to be quite normal below the belt in those days. So my question is, can it be because I masturbate, and would my larger vaginal lips revert to their 'normal' size again if I stopped?

Do you think a man would be shocked and scared if he saw them? It's really my biggest problem. I've never dared go to bed with a man because of my 'abnormal' vaginal lips.

Is it actually so very 'abnormal'? Or is it quite common? I've been all through your ABZ of Love without coming across the phenomenon. As I say, the only place I've come across it is in Love Without Fear.

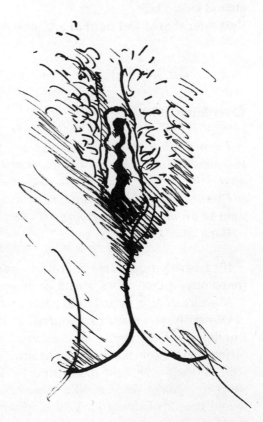

Many girls and women are afraid their sexual organs may become deformed if they masturbate. There's just no cause for worry at all. An American gynaecologist once told us he found it difficult to remember people's *faces*. But when they were stretched out on the couch and he saw the other end he was able to say: 'Why, if it isn't Mrs Smith!'

Because we all look different. So do men's genital organs—not that it should frighten anybody.

Otherwise I feel well and healthy and not the slightest bit abnormal, so you'll be able to help me a lot if you answer my letter.

It seems as if the 'Without Fear' part unfortunately didn't quite tally.

We're afraid we must be disloyal towards a colleague and say that what you have read is just nonsense. Lots of women look just the way you do. Try to see for yourself at a public bath-house. And it has got nothing whatsoever to do with masturbating or not masturbating. Masturbation isn't the slightest bit harmful. Masturbation is completely harmless. Let us add that men don't know very much about what women look like, or should look like.

So you should feel normal and healthy in every single way.

i. & s.h.

Overdoing It?

I have masturbated often and regularly for many years, and this bad habit has resulted in a reduction of the pleasure I get out of an orgasm by fifty to seventy-five per cent.

I've just made the acquaintance of a sweet girl and very much want to avoid spoiling anything with her.

What shall I do?

If masturbation were harmful—particularly if practised frequently—plenty of us would be complaining just like you.

Masturbation is entirely harmless and cannot be overdone.

Obviously you *could* run yourself to death—if you ran from London to Edinburgh, for instance. Obviously, you could distend your stomach in an unhealthy fashion if you tried to stuff yourself with four roast turkeys. Why does nobody ever warn us against dangers like these? Simply because nobody would dream of doing it. You stop when you find you can't manage any more.

So it's absolute rubbish to say—and it still keeps on turning up in books of sexual enlightenment—that masturbation is harmless as long as it isn't 'practised to excess' as they often put it. It's a quite unnecessary thing to add, and only serves to create uneasiness, because we all believe that perhaps we *do* overdo it a bit.

Well then. Your problem cannot stem from masturbation or from too much masturbation—but possibly from anxiety or a feeling of guilt, or a bad conscience? There was a chap who was at university with me who claimed he was utterly incapable of work if he had masturbated in the morning. He said he would have to stay in bed for the rest of the day. And he did, too.

Rubbish, of course, but he believed it—and the sheer fact of believing it really did make him feel fagged out.

People have been put through strength tests before and after masturbation. It turned out that they *felt* fagged out, weak and incapable of doing anything, but in point of fact they were able to perform the same strength tests, even just after ejaculating.

And incidentally, it puts you in such a good mood, makes you feel so relaxed—as long as you don't believe any of the nonsense.

Congratulations on the new girl-friend!

s.h.

Incapable

I've lived without intimate relations with women for a long time and will readily concede that I have often masturbated. In my imagination I can conjure up all manner of exciting situations and easily have an orgasm.

The real thing's a bit different. If I find myself in the same situation in practice, I am incapable of either an erection or an orgasm.

In the course of my travels round Europe I have tried visiting places where you can purchase sexual intercourse, for money. The girls are only too willing, but the results are quite negative. The girls in question have had beautiful bodies and been very active.

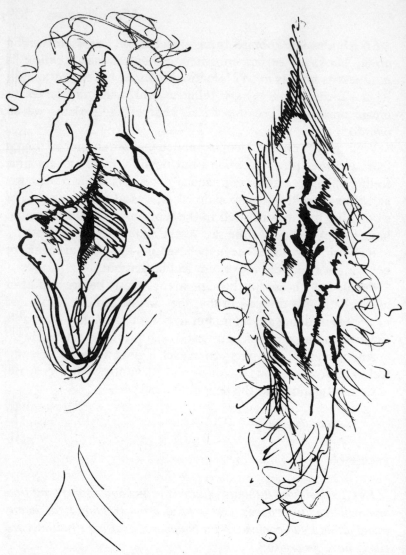

Detailed drawings of the female sexual organs have been spread round this book for two reasons.

1. So that women can have a chance of studying those of other women in close-up. (Don't despair if yours looks different. The idea is to show how different we all are—at this end as well.)

2. So that men can get used to seeing how normal women look. Before sleeping with a woman for the first time a man has seldom seen a grown woman's genital organs at close quarters—so it's not surprising they look a little strange to him.

So I've gradually been getting a bit of a complex about it. I'm afraid of retiring into my own shell and living alone for the rest of my life.

Do you think I could be one of the old-fashioned types to whom things like falling in love and the ringing of bells are necessary ingredients?

You 'concede' that you masturbate. You don't need to concede it. Of course you do—or else you have nocturnal emissions—popularly known as 'wet dreams'.

You should take your basic problem to a good psychoanalyst. Some people are only able to 'perform' with prostitutes, in other words when they are paying for it, and in your case it is possibly the other way round, which is of course better. But some sort of blockage, misunderstanding, anxiety or the like seems to exist which is hard to clear up by correspondence.

i. & s.h.

Suicide No Solution

I'm a girl of eighteen and very unhappy. I've never mentioned my problem to anybody yet, but now I've simply got to know or I'll go crazy. I do so hope you'll answer me. My problem is that I just don't feel a thing when I go to bed with a man. I don't get anything at all out of it, but it feels much better when I masturbate. There's just no comparison, and surely that's not the way things are supposed to be. Unfortunately I still masturbate. I've done it ever since I was quite small. If only I'd never started! Not long ago I got terribly scared because I read in a book: 'Masturbation is not regarded as abnormal as long as it is not preferred to intercourse proper.' Is that really true? If so I'm very unhappy.

I've gone steady with quite a number of boys, but never for very long. Nearly all my girl-friends are engaged. And then I think it's funny it's never hurt me, isn't it supposed to be quite painful the first time? And then I'm very unhappy because my breasts are so small. Is there anything one can do about it? I don't think other

girls have the same problems as I have. I've tried to commit
suicide twice, but it's no solution. Do you think it would help if I
gave up masturbating completely? Do please answer me. You give
so many good answers to others. Am I doomed never to experience
complete happiness with a man?

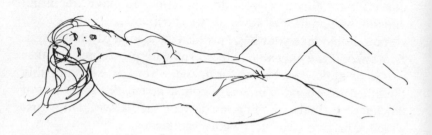

It's dreadful to think that there are still so many people who,
like yourself, are deeply unhappy about something which
shouldn't be a problem at all.

The trouble is that you've never been given proper information about sex—and that by far the majority of men don't know
a thing about women.

We get many letters like yours. Many girls flutter round in a
lost way from one man to the next hoping to experience The
Real Thing. They could have been spared a good deal if they
had been given sensible information about what is normal for a
man and what is normal for a woman.

It's quite common and completely normal to get more out of
masturbation than out of ordinary intercourse. It's the same for
most women—especially when they're young.

It is the sensitive organ called the clitoris, placed just above
the entrance to the vagina, that switches on a woman's sexual
satisfaction, or orgasm. But this switch is seldom influenced
sufficiently during ordinary intercourse. Most men are unaware

of this. Most men assume that a woman's sensations of pleasure start up inside the vagina. They judge—wrongly—by themselves.

When women masturbate, they do so by tickling the clitoris. They don't need to put anything inside the vagina itself, which is what most men believe. Of course many women prefer masturbation to intercourse, because it means the clitoris is tickled in just the right place.

Men who are understanding, imaginative and skilful know this secret—which shouldn't be a secret at all. Of course it gives them a little extra power over the girls they manage to delight— and it's a bit unfair, because any man can learn to become a wonderful lover if he understands what we've just said about the mechanics of sexual pleasure in the woman. Apparently it's rather hard to understand, because you must have read it already if you read books on sex, which you must do as you quote from one.

You will also have read that the first time you sleep with a man need not be painful at all. And even if it does hurt, it seldom hurts very much. But this hasn't sunk in either. Don't you think you ought to take up your studies again?

Let us add that masturbation is an excellent way of obtaining sexual satisfaction. When you find somebody with whom you can have a lovely time together, masturbation fades somewhat into the background. But what they used to say in the old days about masturbation being harmful is complete nonsense. On the contrary, it's a very good way of getting to know yourself. And it's also a very good kind of valve for releasing the pressure which keeps on building up.

It's also nonsense to say that masturbation is only normal amongst children, young people or unmarried people. Masturbation occurs in happy marriages too.

We've answered your questions in detail because we know these things have to be said many times. You are completely normal and have just the same chances as all other girls of—as you put it—experiencing complete happiness with a man.

i. & s.h.

No Men, Thank You!

Would you please help a woman of over forty? I've had nothing to do with men sexually for almost fifteen years, and have no desire to either, nor with women.

Instead, about once a week, I've used a finger, but it doesn't completely satisfy me.

I've often thought of buying a rubber penis and then hope for better results—or one of those electric vibrators, but I daren't go into the kind of shop that sells them.

How do you use a vibrator, on the outside? Or can you get it inside your vagina? Or would a rubber penis be better? Roughly how much do these things cost? I'm not very well off, so they mustn't be too expensive.

In the past I've laughed whenever anyone said I couldn't go on being normal if I never had any sex with men, but I'm beginning to agree with them now.

Can it harm you in any way to use a rubber penis or a vibrator? Hope you won't laugh at me.

There's no question of our laughing—because you have outlined, honestly and sensibly, some of the problems many single women ponder over.

We've often stressed the importance of titillating the clitoris —and the area round it—because masses of men know nothing whatsoever about it. That's why we've also advised against attaching too much importance to the sensation of a penis inside the vagina—from the woman's viewpoint, that is—because she seldom finds it enough.

On the other hand we don't want to suggest that a woman can't have any sensations and feelings inside her vagina. Of course she can. Particularly since the penis pushes against the smaller vaginal lips, which continue upwards to form a foreskin round the clitoris. And of course women can feel and enjoy having a penis inside their vagina—some more than others. Others very little.

We're writing all this because we don't want you to expect too much from a rubber penis.

Various kinds of rubber penis are available, at various prices, but we believe an ordinary irrigator (see the illustration), consisting of a red rubber bulb and a black plastic tube, would give you just as much pleasure—though it's possible that the mere *sight* of a rubber penis would play a part. But an irrigator would certainly be cheaper and easier to buy. The thickness isn't important. The female vagina can allow the passage of baby's

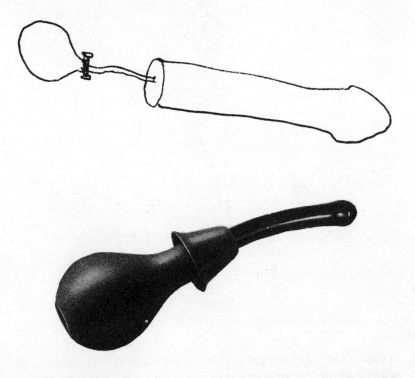

Above—A solidly made, closed rubber condom in penis form. Designed to be pumped up with the help of the bulb at the end, which has a valve so that it can be closed off.

Below—An irrigator.

head, but it can also close firmly round a thin pencil. Irrigators can be bought at chemists and rubber goods shops.

Electric vibrators are obtainable from electrical shops—sometimes chemists—in many sizes and operate at various

An electric massager can naturally be used in any place.

speeds. They are supplied either as battery-driven models or with leads to be plugged into the mains. (See our *Consumer Guide.*) The battery-driven models in particular can be inserted into the vagina, but they are mainly intended for titillating the clitoris and the region surrounding it.

Mini-vibrators (battery-driven) are no bigger than a lipstick.

Larger vibrators, penis-shaped, also made of plastic, are available with two speeds, also battery-driven.

Then there are the vibrators designed for massage proper, complete with various gadgets for use all over the body (but not for pushing inside the vagina), a lead and adjustable to various speeds (usually between two and four). But a simple kind is cheaper.

There are many dealers, and most of them will happily send their wares COD, or to a *poste restante* address if the agreed amount has been paid in advance.

There's nothing harmful at all in using the things you have in mind—on the contrary. You're not going dotty, but it's probably nicest for most people to find someone else to be lonely with. Why have you completely given up?

i. & s.h.

6. Special Problems

This chapter is a mixed bag into which we've put a whole lot of questions that didn't fit into the other chapters. *Special problems* thus does not necessarily imply that one is something special, a unique case—even though we have put certain minorities and special wishes in this 'bag'.

What is 'normal' covers a wide range, and most of us have our own little whims in the sphere of sex—perhaps shared by only a few hundred thousand others on this earth. This applies, for instance, to people who like rubberwear, or men who like wearing female clothes once in a while. (Girls can do so quite freely—wear men's clothes, we mean—without ever discovering that they are transvestites.) It applies to men who like being beaten (and who sometimes also like to beat, but are seldom allowed to).

Many men like to see sexy underwear. Some like to see it on women—others like to put it on themselves as well. Some, as already mentioned, like rubberwear.

Silky Soft and Pale Pink

I'm a young man of almost thirty. Unfortunately I have a dreadful perversion. I'm simply crazy about wearing ladies' panties —I like them to be soft and pale pink and silky.

I'd like to ask you, Inge, what you feel personally. Do you think I'll ever find a woman who will accept this?

What also happens to me is that I get a terrific erection the moment I see a woman in pale pink underwear.

You've got your little eccentricity—which you actually share with quite a lot of other people.

We're convinced you could find a number of women who

would take your speciality quite calmly—but it also depends a little on whether you yourself can get as far as accepting it.

You've probably already read in our column about the Swedish club for men who sometimes dress up in female clothing from top to toe, including wigs, cosmetics, etc. These men have a far more difficult time—it's also a very impractical business. They often have wives who have completely accepted the situation.

You're not as eccentric as the man who went to a psychiatrist and said: 'My wife has sent me. She says I'm crazy because I'm so fond of fried eggs.'

'That sounds a bit peculiar,' said the nerve specialist. 'There's nothing crazy about that. I love fried eggs!'

'Really?' said the man delightedly. 'Would you like a couple then? I've got two suitcases full of them.'

i.h.

The Sweat Runs off Him

My husband likes to put on my girdle, stockings and panties. He's done it before when I wasn't at home, but now he's told me and asked if he can do it when I'm at home too. He wears his own clothes on top, but it doesn't give him an orgasm.

He says it's a strong desire he feels, and so he's got to do something about it, but it makes him feel ashamed.

Sometimes he likes to have intercourse with me when he's wearing my things, but then he likes it to be the other way round first, i.e. 'sixty-nine', with the tongue, and then the normal way, and then he soon has an ejaculation, but not before he knows I've come.

When we're lying sixty-nine I can see how his testicles and scrotum sort of disappear completely. Is it unnatural? We're forty.

He feels like a man and wants to be a man. But he's had this thing about women's clothes ever since he was a little boy. We've been to see the doctor, and he told us not to worry. But he had to give us some nerve pills, because we can't help worrying.

My husband has never wanted to have anything to do with his own sex, on the contrary, but it upsets him badly. He tries to resist the longing, and the perspiration stands out on his forehead when it comes over him, but it's something that gives him great pleasure and in the end he can't help doing it.

If only you could help us!

You've got an extremely sensible doctor and you should listen to him. And you should be happy your husband has dared to confide his problem to you.

Now you must be sensible enough to play too, and help him to accept it. It's a great compliment to you, and we see no reason why he should stop doing it if it amuses him.

It doesn't hurt him, or you, or anybody else.

Other people have their little peculiarities in this respect, and in most cases it's completely harmless. It has got nothing to do with homosexuality, but has a nice scientific name, *transvestism*, if you absolutely have to give it a label. And a very mild example of it at that.

Lots of women feel the same desire to wear men's clothing, but then it's not forbidden, so they can just do it—without ever as much as realizing it's a sexual speciality.

Lots of men put on one or more items of female clothing *for fun* without ever thinking that it's actually an offshoot of the same desire. So there's not the slightest reason to feel ashamed.

i. & s.h.

In Women's Clothing

I too have read with great interest about men who, without being homosexual, have an irresistible desire to dress up in women's clothing once in a while.

It's just the same with me. I'm a man, thirty-five years of age. Ever since I was a boy I've had a desire to wear girl's clothes. I've fought and struggled against it, and above all I've been alone with my problem. Can one get 'cured'?

It comes over me in periods. Particularly at full moon, as far as I've been able to observe. Could there be something in this?

On the one hand I'm delighted to hear about the club that has been formed by men with similar interests, for it must be marvellous to be able to meet others and for the first time in one's life talk about it quite openly to them.

On the other hand I'm afraid of being unmasked. I have quite an important job and am probably regarded as what I believe Ibsen called a pillar of society. It would be ruinous for me, for my family and in particular a shock for my wife if anything were to come out about my special tastes.

We've had several letters like yours, and we know that quite a number of people either have or will apply to the Swedish club. Amongst the members there are a number of men in so-called top jobs, and great importance is attached to discretion.

We've met most of them, and found them intelligent and pleasant. For all of them it has been a colossal relief to be able to get together and talk about it—to be able to go out together wearing women's clothes and all the rest of it, as you can well imagine.

We have already heard about the desire making itself felt at full moon, but whether it's common and what connection there may be in it we cannot say. Some feel the desire once in six months, others every week.

In the transvestite club three types of wife are distinguished.

A-wives, who know all about their husbands' special wishes and who completely accept them. Some go out with them and buy female clothing and generally take the whole thing as a huge joke which the two of them share—and who virtually feel they've got themselves a husband and a girl-friend in one and the same person.

B-wives, who know about it all right, but prefer to be kept out of it.

C-wives, who know nothing—as a rule because the husband has reason to suspect that his wife just won't be able to take it.

In a few cases this suspicion is unfounded, but the husband doesn't dare take the chance.

In this connection we may add that it's probably best if one can confide in one's wife before getting married. We've seen several examples of A-wives, and it has been a real pleasure.

We can't help heaving a little sigh at the fact that the club is so fanatically reserved for heterosexual transvestites, for homosexuals who like wearing women's clothing have just as great a need for support. But we appreciate that there are various practical reasons which make strict segregation necessary. Yet amongst all men and women, the difference between heterosexuality and homosexuality isn't nearly as marked as society fanatically tries to make it. We are probably all capable of reacting sexually to both the one sex and the other. We are thus all to a certain extent bi-sexual. (As a matter of fact we are born bi-sexual.) Some of us have succumbed to the fear displayed by society and convinced ourselves that we're only capable of sexual relationships with the other sex; and others, for some reason or other, have had some sort of mental block and believe they can only have sexual relationships with persons of the same sex.

The Club is thus keeping up the prejudices, but, as we say, we understand the reasons.

i. & s.h.

Man or Woman?

One reads in the papers these days about sportsmen and sportswomen being examined. In point of fact I understand it's the women who get examined to make sure they really are women.
How do they do it?

The sex of a person can be determined in three ways:
1. You can tell by the genital organs. As a rule it is quite clear, but there are thousands of hermaphrodites whose sex is hard to tell just by looking at their genitals.

2. By examining a cell from the person in question under the microscope it is possible to count the chromosomes and thus determine the sex. It is the most decisive and least doubtful method. There are only two possibilities, man or woman—and this is the test used on sportswomen.

3. Finally, you can ask the person in question outright. This may sound silly, but the main thing from the viewpoint of the person concerned is 'Do I feel myself to be a man or a woman?' And this is a question which only the person concerned can answer.

So it's a very complicated question, because there are people who, according to either the first or the second method, clearly belong to the one sex, but feel they belong to the other.

There are women who, anatomically speaking, are women, insofar that vagina, clitoris, womb and ovaries are all there, but who deny that they are women, consistently demand to be addressed as Mr, wear man's clothing, have their hair cut like a man and do a man's job at their place of work, where they are quite simply taken for men.

There are men who have a penis and testicles and sperm, but who, with or without permission from the police, go round dressed as women and in all outward respects behave like women. This is not the same thing as homosexuality, even though some of those who have passed over to the other sex— and likewise known as transvestites—may be homosexual.

Sounds confusing, doesn't it? It certainly is. And it can be tragic for those affected. It can't be very funny, for instance, for the woman sprinter who is suddenly declared to be a man on radio and TV stations all over the world and has all her gold medals taken away from her. It isn't likely that he/she has slyly intended to deceive the whole world of sport. What seems to be involved is a person who has felt herself to be a woman and perhaps also anatomically, according to method No 1, is a woman, but according to the chromosome count is a man.

And then there is the story of the old lady who was brought in to see her great-grandchild, who lay stark naked in a cradle, kicking away.

'Is it a boy or a girl?' asked the old lady.

'But great-grandma, can't you see?' asked the young parents.

'It's not my sight that's failing me,' said the old lady, 'it's my memory.'

A funny but rather foolish story, because fortunately most people remember very clearly on this point to the end of their days.

i. & s.h.

Untruthful Pornography

Does the amount of liquid secreted at the moment of orgasm vary from one woman to the next? When my husband and I have intercourse, virtually no moisture comes at the moment of orgasm —or at most a single drop. But my husband says it still feels the same as with other women.

In the few pornographic books I have read they always talk about a veritable gush!

Oh yes! All these untruthful pornographic books! As a rule they are written by men and deal with men's daydreams about women, and are thus never honest descriptions of men's experiences with women. Unfortunately they serve to fill a lot of people with inferiority complexes.

(Let's make one thing clear: pornography is excellent if it is used as a means of sexual stimulation and is not taken for anything more than it is, namely a better means than hormone injections administered by a doctor—cheaper, easier, better and more fun. But lies and daydreams. Let's hope that honest descriptions of sexual relationships will come soon.)

Now then. Women do not secrete any moisture, in fact no liquid at all, at the moment of orgasm. It's a very widespread superstition and one that is hard to eradicate from people's minds—for, of course, moisture is secreted during the period leading up to the orgasm, i.e. a lubricant is secreted in the vagina as the woman becomes more and more excited. And some women 'lubricate' more than others. But there's still nothing corresponding to a man's ejaculation of sperm at the moment of orgasm.

i. & s.h.

Orgasmic Secretion

My otherwise angelic husband came dashing in and showed me your answer on the subject of women's orgasmic secretions—what an expression!

You really mustn't turn me into pornography or authors' fantasies, because women exist who really do have secretions of this kind—and have to use a piece of plastic under the sheet. And can never make love in a strange bed. It'd get ruined!

I don't mind telling you two dear people that my eyes, which are blue, go even bluer, all shining and happy, and my voice, my whole person, radiates joy and happiness when the time comes round again when my husband pulls himself together and makes love to me.

You mustn't try to console the masses by saying that something is pornographic or wrong if it's at the expense of individuals. I have my doctor's word for it that I'm not a common case, but that I'm certainly not abnormal—worth a fortune to the right man!

So once more you've spoilt something that I've tried to take naturally, and the worst thing about it is that my husband now believes there's something wrong, because now he's seen it put down in black and white.

Now he thinks I'm the one with the wrong ideas, and that I demand something I don't really need.

I've asked my doctor to give me something to counteract my strong desires, but he just says he doesn't serve roast pork and cabbage to new-born babes. Do pills of this kind actually exist?

We're terribly sorry if we've spoilt anything for you, and hope you will forgive us. But we actually believe you're confusing a number of different things.

We did state quite clearly that some women 'lubricate' more than others. But we repeat: there is no question of any orgasmic secretion as with a man. But there is a lubricant that is secreted by the woman as her sexual excitement increases—and the greater the excitement the greater the amount.

But we haven't labelled it pornography, or wrong—on the contrary, it's lovely—even though it can be a bit impractical, as you yourself mention. We quite agree with your doctor that you're unusually lovely—but then it's not normal to be unusual. What *is* pornographic and wrong is that certain authors, who also think it's lovely, untruthfully claim that ordinary women are like that. This gives all the lovely, ordinary girls inferiority complexes—that is, if they're told that a girl should get as fantastically wet as you apparently do.

Other girls can perfectly well get bluer eyes and radiate joy and happiness and have a marvellous sex life without necessarily requiring a plastic groundsheet.

What seems to be your problem is that your husband doesn't pull himself together often enough—and that he's not delighted with his unusual wife.

We haven't helped to reduce this problem, and we are sorry about it, but it seems to have been there even without our answer to the other letter you mention.

You've asked your doctor for some form of sedative that can pacify your strong desires. Such pills don't exist. Apart from which we don't actually understand your doctor's answer. He should have said that perhaps your husband was in need of advice and guidance—to help him turn into 'the right man'—the chap to whom you really are worth a fortune. Not on account of the plastic sheeting, but because you attach such great value to sexual relations.

In other words, the trouble seems to be that your husband feels he is pressed to do more than he can manage—and then he tries to defend himself by saying that you're the one who's abnormal, overdemanding, etc. Instead, he ought to learn some forms of sexual technique that would place him in a position to meet the demands which he now thinks he can't meet. It can be done, but of course it demands an effort on your part too.

It means that both you and he must be prepared to experiment —and to accept each other. In particular, he must accept you.

i. & s.h.

PS. Others have also written to us about women who get unusually wet. Some women do. We've never denied it.

Just a Drop

My problem isn't a very big one, because I'm very happily married, have a lovely sex life and a kind husband.

The only thing I'd like to know is whether it's normal, in the course of my orgasm, to pee a little—I just can't help it, even if I've recently emptied my bladder.

Neither of us is squeamish, but thinking about it beforehand tends to hold me back a bit, because I think it's a bit indelicate.

Most women don't, but we've often heard of it—and it's one of the things that has given rise to the myth about women having a kind of ejaculation corresponding to that of a man.

You will find inferior pornographic stories that describe how 'the love juices sprayed forth from between his mistress's thighs like a fountain.' But this is a foolish and romanticized superstition. Many women haven't dared tell their proud males about the little drop they didn't manage to hold back.

In reality it's actually a compliment to him that your orgasm is so wonderful, abandoned and relaxing that even the ring muscle—the muscle which closes the exit from the bladder—is able to relax a little.

You shouldn't let it distract you. Urine is actually one of the purest, most sterile liquids we know—when fresh.

Accept this and say to yourself and your husband: What a lucky girl I am!

i. & s.h.

I Can't Bring Myself to Do It

*My husband and I have lived together for eight years now, and
we actually suit each other very well sexually, but there's one
thing that bothers me a little.*

*A couple of years ago, while we were having intercourse, my
husband asked me to do something for him. It wasn't anything
difficult, or tiring, or anything that hurts, or in any other way
unpleasant, but it scared me—and I just couldn't bring myself
to do it.*

*We talked about it afterwards and he apologized for having
asked me to do it, but he'd been thinking about it for a long time
and it was something he wished very badly. We haven't talked
about it since, but I have thought about it a great deal, and have
actually tried and tried to be more broadminded, but it's somehow
against my nature, or my upbringing.*

*The unfortunate thing is that, as a result, I no longer dare to be
so relaxed when we make love together nowadays as I would like
to be—and am actually able to be. I feel restrained by a fear that
he may ask me to do something or other that I won't be able to
bring myself to do.*

*I've also tried to adjust myself to his way of thinking, but
somehow cannot rest content with my own opinion. It's not a thing
I care to ask anybody except you about.*

*Please answer me quite honestly. Is it quite in order that we
should be this way? My husband says that whatever two people
decide to do together is perfectly all right and natural, but
supposing I don't happen to find it right?*

We have quoted your letter here—in slightly shortened form
—because the same problem crops up in nearly all marriages.
The man or the wife gets a bright idea, but his or her partner
shies away and wonders: Is it natural? Is it perverted? (And
unfortunately one idea soon gives way to the next!)

Your husband is right. It's got nothing to do with anybody
else what two people decide to do together. And your case is a
trifling one compared with what goes on in many marriages.

Your husband's proposal (which we have deliberately left to our readers' imaginations, for it is really immaterial in this connection) is—as is often the case—an idea which he happens to regard as exciting and which doesn't cost you anything. You just can't trust your emotions in such matters. Fortunately! Otherwise marital relations would often be very boring.

Life isn't so simple, people aren't as superficial and easy to understand as one often thinks. Marriage isn't a boring row of pearls on a string. A little variation and inventiveness is required.

i. & s.h.

Are All Latins Like This?

'Happiness is knowing what is normal,' you write. Is this normal:

My sweet little niece has become engaged to a southerner. They are living together and will soon be getting married, but now she tells me in a moment of confidence that she has been wondering if it's the right thing after all, because he has begun to make sexual demands on her which she does not wish to meet.

What gives him the greatest satisfaction, for instance, is anal coition. She finds it both unaesthetic and revolting, in fact it practically makes her sick, she gets giddy and everything goes black. He also insists on her masturbating while he watches her. She doesn't care for this in the slightest, as she derives full sexual satisfaction in the normal way.

She fully realizes (because she has studied books on sexual enlightenment) that what both partners feel like doing together isn't necessarily perverted.

What advice can I give her?

The same thing happened to me a few years ago with an extremely cultured man of about fifty. I myself am this age, and no novice, but I'd never come up against that sort of demand before, and I didn't care for it either, so I had to break off the relationship.

Is it a typical Latin trait, my niece asks, and I ask whether it's the sort of thing that only arises in Nordic males when their sexual potency is beginning to ebb?

The bounds of 'normalcy' are very wide. Neither Latins nor elderly Nordic males hold any patent for thinking up various kinds of fun in bed.

Anal coition and a man liking to watch a woman masturbating are by no means uncommon. (Anal intercourse between husband and wife is actually illegal in some countries, including Britain.) But, of course, it requires the acquiescence of both parties. If one is disgusted by something, the other must renounce the pleasure. On the other hand there are women who are disgusted by quite banal sexual things, and if one always complied with the wishes of such women there wouldn't be much left.

It is difficult to give your niece straightforward advice, but she shouldn't agree to much more than she feels she can cope with.

i. & s.h.

A Girl's Uncle

Is it incest to be in love with my mother's half-brother? He's the son of my mother's father, but not with my grandmother, just with another woman.

If you stick to just being in love it doesn't matter who the person is. It's not until some form of sex play comes into the picture that the law of most countries takes a hand.

Parents are not allowed to have intercourse with their children, brothers and sisters are not allowed to have intercourse with each other. But a mother's half-brother is all right.

Half-uncles and even whole uncles are in season all year round.

They are stricter about these matters in Finland, where

cousins are not allowed to have intercourse with each other. But France, Russia and Italy (to pick a few examples) have a more liberal outlook on the matter than, for instance, the Danes.

i. & s.h.

Brother and Sister

Could you give us your advice in connection with a dreadful affair?

Recently we caught our fourteen-year-old son and our twelve-year-old daughter in a very intimate situation. We were naturally very shocked and my wife flew off the handle and gave both of them such a beating that I had to intervene.

We've all got on so well otherwise. They're generally the sweetest children you could imagine, helpful and pleasant in every way and good at their lessons. Everybody likes them.

What shall we do?

My wife is quite beside herself and wants to hand them over to the Child Welfare authorities—but I think it's a terrible idea. It would ruin our lives completely, as we'd virtually lose them for many years—probably for life, as they would be bound to feel bitter towards us.

But seeing it's an incestuous relationship, I suppose there's nothing else we can do?

Yes, by heavens, there is!

You've already done a great deal. You've made it quite clear to your children that it is something society regards very severely. You've done this pretty forcibly. Much too forcibly.

It so happens there's nearly always a very marked difference between a society's official moral code and what people actually do. It must be said, in all fairness, that it's certainly not unusual (and all those who have had brothers and sisters know this) for things of one kind and another to take place, to a greater or lesser extent, amongst children.

We think your wife has taken the whole affair much too seriously. We also regard it in a much milder light than you do.

We are fully convinced that your children have now been very forcibly made aware of society's outlook on the subject. We feel you and your wife should now try to forget about it completely. We're sure you have a couple of very sweet and intelligent children who aren't the slightest bit worse than so many other sweet children. And you needn't have any fears about the future!

Nor should you start spying on your children, or checking up on their comings and goings, or let them think you don't trust them. If you do, you'll lose their confidence completely.

i. & s.h.

Mother and Son

I am forty and my mother is fifty-five, so she had me when she was only fifteen. When I was about ten or twelve, my father was often away for a couple of weeks or so, and sometimes my mother would lie down and fondle me. Then she'd have an orgasm, and I too experienced a sweet pain.

My mother and father were divorced later—not on account of her 'affair' with me—after which our relationship developed in earnest.

My mother is a very beautiful and robust woman. We love each other and could not imagine living without each other. Some time ago we went to a party which ended up by everybody swapping wives. My mother and I went home instead.

What do you think? Is it a sin that we love each other? We don't do anybody any harm by it.

We can't live without each other. Of course we realize it's illegal, that it's incest, but our mutual love is so great that it rejects all laws. We'd rather die.

Let's agree that the situation you've ended up in is not only impractical but also a very special one.

It is not our task to moralize, nor to decide what is sinful and what is not. We can only repeat what you yourself realize: it is an illegal situation.

There are reasonable laws, and there are unreasonable ones. The law concerning incest is designed to preserve the peace in families so that sons and daughters and fathers and mothers can live together without disturbing factors.

Your personal situation, involving a very young mother and a frequently absent father, explains a good deal.

It's not a thing we can recommend. It can very easily become too great a strain for both persons.

i. & s.h.

My Sister

I too have a sexual problem that makes me feel ashamed. For the past couple of years or so I've been sleeping with my sister, although we're both married and have grown-up children.

My wife doesn't know anything about it, nor does her husband. We've sworn not to tell anybody anything, but we are so happy.

Should we stop? Have you heard of similar cases?

Of course we've heard of brothers and sisters who have got together in various ways. It's not so unusual, but it generally stops when those concerned find their own mates.

Society passes severe judgement in such cases, which is why not so very much is heard about them. It is called *incest*, and there's a certain amount of superstition to the effect that a relationship of this sort will produce deformed children.

This fear is highly exaggerated. Only if there happens to be a particularly unfortunate genetic factor in the family is there any risk that such factors may be clearly pronounced in any children of the relationship.

This may also be the case if two people from different families but with the same genetic factor have children together.

The law against closely related persons going to bed with each other is based more on the fact that it can create disturbances in the family. It's not so good if the son chucks the father out and starts co-habiting with the mother. And it's not exactly a good thing to have the father chuck the mother out and take over the daughters instead.

This is the real background for it.

In your case you create no more disturbance or upset than if you were unfaithful to your wife with anybody else. But of course—just as in all other cases—the best and most desirable thing would be if you could revert to enjoying life with your respective marital partners—but no doubt this is what you feel already?

i. & s.h.

Foursome

Two years ago my wife and I were let down by our good friends, of whom we were very fond. Perhaps we had grown weary of each other.

We were upset about it, but got over it. And then, not so long ago, we had a reunion, and were so happy to be in each other's company again that we ended up by going to bed with each other's wives. It had never happened before, but it was marvellous and lasted two whole days.

But now I've got the most awful conscience about it. I simply can't forget it and have lost all desire for my wife, food and everything.

What shall I do?

Presumably your wives also went to bed with each other's husbands? You say nothing about what your wife felt or feels. Or your friends?

Of course it was marvellous. Ideas of this kind probably churn round in the minds of most people. And one day, when birth control and venereal diseases are no longer a problem, we'll be brought up in a way that'll make us take unfaithfulness more lightly.

We're afraid of supporting group sex at the moment because we've seen examples which seem to indicate that we—our generation—just can't take it.

Perhaps your problem is that your wife enjoyed herself too much? Somebody usually draws a short straw (perhaps more than one person) when two or more couples start frolicking together.

But what is done is done, and perhaps the damage is not irreparable. It should be possible for grown-up people to get together and say: 'Listen, it was fun, but it's likely to get a bit risky in the long run. Let's stop while the going is good and carry on being good friends.'

i. & s.h.

Triangular Affairs and Wife-Swapping

I can remember your writing that one day we'd get as far as taking marital infidelity with equanimity. I've tried it, and I don't think you're right.

You've misunderstood us. We said that when unwanted children and venereal diseases have been abolished, a basis will be provided to enable us—i.e. the coming generations—to regard the question of marital infidelity more lightly. But we generally add that we—that is to say you and ourselves—are not mature enough for it yet. Our generation is unlikely to be so.

At all events we've seen many instances of people who have tried it, but in each case it's only worked for a while. Then one of those involved has been unable to stand it any longer.

We can tell you a real-life story from a kindergarten. Five-year-old Willy confided to his mother: 'Mummy, I would so like to marry Jeanette, but she's awfully fond of Peter, so I'll probably have to marry him too!'

i. & s.h.

A Married Virgin

We've been married for five years now, and during this time my husband and I have never been to bed with each other properly. Our marriage has never been 'consummated', as they say—I'm much too scared and afraid.

My husband has been terribly sweet and patient, but I'm afraid it must get on his nerves most dreadfully.

Time and again I've decided, 'Well, this time!' But every time I get terrified, tense all my muscles—and then it's hopeless. I got married late, and I have an idea what is at the bottom of it all.

I grew up in a home where anything to do with sex was disgusting. I love my husband, and I would understand if he wanted to sleep with other women. It so happens he doesn't. I've been to see my doctor, but he doesn't really understand me.

He passed me on to a gynaecologist, who offered to break my virginity with a murderous-looking instrument, but I didn't dare let him.

Dear i. and s.h., help me to save my marriage before it's too late!

We have received letters like yours before, so you're certainly not the only one to have this problem.

There are people who claim in a superior fashion that 'it's something any animal and any damned fool can find out how to do', and of course there's something in that, but we *human beings* happen to be very strongly marked by our so-called civilization, which includes our upbringing, and most of us can experience difficulty in behaving in a completely natural way.

A book has been written by L. J. Friedman entitled *Virgin Wives* and published in 1962 in a series called *Mind and Medicine Monographs*. It deals with a hundred English women who, like yourself, had been married for a number of years but were still virgins. Seventy of these women (in other words seventy per cent) were treated successfully and were thereafter capable of normal intercourse. One woman had been married for seventeen years, and the treatment was so successful she found she was able to make love with her husband several times a week afterwards.

The book advises very strongly against artificial breaking of virginity. In nearly all cases what is really behind the trouble is a form of mental block, i.e. something psychic, a very powerful sense of fear, as in your case—and fear cannot be removed by force.

The method of treatment that produces the best results seem to be conversations with a sensible and clever psychologist or nerve specialist. Good progress can be made after relatively few conversations.

It often turns out that a woman has a completely mistaken impression of her own anatomy. The simple fact of learning a bit more about one's own body and internal organs can be a useful thing.

We would also recommend you to examine yourself very thoroughly. Get hold of a couple of books on female anatomy. Try (and perhaps let your husband try too, later) to push a finger up into your vagina, and after that two, and then three, so as to convince yourself that there really is room.

You don't mention the question of having children. Your fear may be due to an exaggerated notion of the nature of birth pains.

It also seems that men are often too nice, too patient. A touch of tactful insistence on the part of the man would also appear to be helpful.

At all events, don't despair. There are good chances of arriving at a more satisfactory solution. Nobody ever achieves a perfect sex life, but you can have a lovely time trying.

i. & s.h.

I Want Rubber

I'm a young woman of twenty-five. Ever since I was confirmed I've been very strongly attracted by things made of rubber—I mean rubber mackintoshes, rubber boots, rubber gloves and so on. It's been rather difficult for me to find men—well, a man—to share my interests and lusts in this direction.

What I enjoy most about rubberwear is quite simply being able to feel, smell and look at it. I also enjoy looking at other people wearing things made of rubber. On a few occasions I've masturbated while watching people wearing things made of rubber.

I wear mackintoshes, rubber boots etc. a lot myself, especially on sexual occasions, but it's not quite enough. When I'm with a man I feel a strong desire to dominate him—and in some way or other it's tied up with my interest in rubberwear.

Can you help me find a solution?

We have come across the interest in rubber only a couple of times before—in men, so it's not so common. It may be a bit difficult to find somebody to share it with. Nevertheless, a man who is fond of you will very quickly be able to share your interest. But it may be a bit difficult amongst people of your own age, who will probably be scared off.

We can't help you, but try putting an advertisement in a magazine and you'll find yourself drowning in letters. We're afraid of doing the same thing at the moment, which is why we have to say quite firmly that we cannot take upon ourselves the task of establishing contacts.

i. & s.h.

Rubberwear Enthusiasts

A little while ago you wrote about a girl who liked rubberwear and suggested that she could try putting an advertisement in a magazine. I quite understand that you can't operate as a 'contact agent' but at the same time it would be nice if there were a place where those of us who belong to sexual minorities could contact each other.

By the way, is there a Latin name for people who like rubberwear?

I'd like to take advantage of your offer to remain anonymous as my husband would be furious if you wrote to me direct. He opens all my letters.

Thanks for your letter. It seems there are far more people interested in rubberwear than we realized.

We haven't the slightest objection to acting as 'contact agents', basically. But it's not quite the point of this column of ours. Every week we receive a couple of hundred queries or so, and we carefully burn all the envelopes and letters once we've answered them. In other words, we have no chance of putting readers in touch with one another. It would require keeping and filing the letters we had answered—and that would clash with our strict rules to the effect that the names and addresses of those who write to ask us something must never come to the knowledge of anybody but ourselves.

It so happens that sexual minorities have a chance of finding contacts in some magazines which accept advertisements of this kind. Where the chances are best we cannot say.

We don't know the Latin name for a sexual interest in rubberwear, but we'll gladly invent one for you: Latexism.

It really shakes us to hear so many women mention that their husbands open their letters! It's against the law and quite apart from that utterly unforgivable.

i. & s.h.

Mackintosh

I've just come home from abroad and see that anybody can write to you and ask you what they want—without even having to give their name and address. I should like to avail myself of this unique opportunity.

I've been living abroad in a big city, where I rented a room from a woman who lived alone with her daughter and a maid. One of the last days I was there something happened which has tormented me ever since. I just can't get it out of my head, and whenever I think of it I get terribly excited.

One evening I'd gone quietly into the living-room to borrow a book from the bookshelf, something which I'd been given permission to do. In the next room, the door of which was ajar, I could hear my landlady and her fourteen- or fifteen-year-old daughter talking loudly. I could hear that the girl's mother was scolding her, and telling her she deserved to be punished on the spot.

So far everything sounded very normal, but then the daughter answered in a very small voice that she was prepared to receive the punishment she deserved. I heard the mother immediately call in the maid and ask her to bring along 'the usual things'.

I know I should have left the room, but something kept me riveted to the spot. The maid came back with a dog-whip, a white dust-coat which she put on herself, and a rubber mackintosh, which the mother put on. Then the mother asked her daughter to get ready.

The maid sat on a chair and pulled up her white dust-coat, and the daughter lay across her lap with her bottom bared. When the mother had buttoned up her mackintosh, she started to beat her daughter with the dog-whip. I watched the whole scene through the crack in the door, because it was dark in the room where I was standing, and the lights were on where they were.

When it was over, the daughter knelt at her mother's feet and kissed her black rubber mackintosh fervently.

Of course I couldn't talk to my landlady about it, and shortly after I left the city.

But since then, whenever I see a woman in a white dust-coat or a rubber mackintosh, I get a terrific erection. The other day I was being served by a young woman in a chemist's shop, and she smiled at me and buttoned a button of her dust-coat—and I had to leave the shop as fast as I could.

What shall I do? Am I abnormal?

You naturally feel your problem is the greatest, and this is perfectly reasonable.

The rest of us can't help thinking of the poor girl who is in the clutches of the other two women. Her sexual urges are going to get twisted in what is, to put it mildly, an unfortunate direction.

When the damage is done, we are the first to encourage those who want to do some beating to get together with those who enjoy being beaten, because then there's little else to do about it. But of course it's better if people aren't influenced in such an abnormal or anomalous direction.

'Perverted' actually means anomalous, and the two women may be termed anomalous, although it's not as unusual as most of us think.

All this moralizing is unlikely to be of much interest to you, but we had to air a little of our concern for this fourteen- or fifteen-year-old girl who is being denied a chance of developing more freely.

You have also been affected by the situation, but not only by what you *saw*. A tendency has lain dormant in you in one way or another, and has only just manifested itself.

Presumably you didn't have a fixed and satisfying relationship yourself while you were staying in this city. You have been susceptible, easily influenced on account of your unsatisfied sexual urges.

Perhaps you yourself were beaten when a child, or in your teens—and if so it's the sort of memory that could have played a part on a quiet evening when, quite unprepared but easily aroused, you were taken by surprise by witnessing this violent scene.

. It is obvious that all three females have had a powerful sexual reward from this punishment, and it's not so often we are obliged to witness other people obtain sexual satisfaction. If one is hungry and sees somebody else eating, one's own hunger can well become more pronounced than ever, and then as a rule it's quite easy to dash along and satisfy this hunger. Perhaps you didn't have this opportunity.

All the above has been an attempt at an explanation. What ought you to do? Well, the problem isn't all that difficult. You must find yourself a girl who will be prepared to sympathize. Perhaps you will be able to persuade her to put on a white dust-coat or a mackintosh? Mackintosh girls do exist, you know.

i. & s.h.

As Nature Intended

I am a woman of fifty-seven years of age, and I'd like to know why you don't strike a good blow for the normal form of intercourse.

It seems to me to be quite crazy that human beings generally make love the wrong way round. I've never seen either mammals or birds throw themselves flat on their backs in order to mate. Surely the only natural way is for the male to insert his penis from behind.

Well, there may be something in it.

There have been natives who were very surprised to see white people in action with the woman lying on her back and the man on top. They had never realized it was possible. They dubbed this form of intercourse 'the missionary position'.

In the days of the ancient Roman Empire it wasn't usual for the woman to lie on her back either. It's only something which we, today, in our Western culture, have adopted as normal.

We don't think that either the missionary position or the one you suggest are particularly good. Admittedly the man can roll the woman's clitoris between finger and thumb when he inserts his penis from behind, and he can fondle the woman's breasts, which can also be of great importance. There are a few women whose clitoris is sufficiently titillated by the movement of the penis against the smaller vaginal lips, but they are exceptions.

If we were to recommend a better position for the woman it would be the one where she sits on top and the man lies on his back. It is a position which gives the woman a better chance of moving and has a couple of other advantages. But it still can't be said to guarantee success.

i. & s.h.

PS. On the right you can see some drawings made by a learned scientist which shows that even a mountain gorilla can be quite imaginative at times.

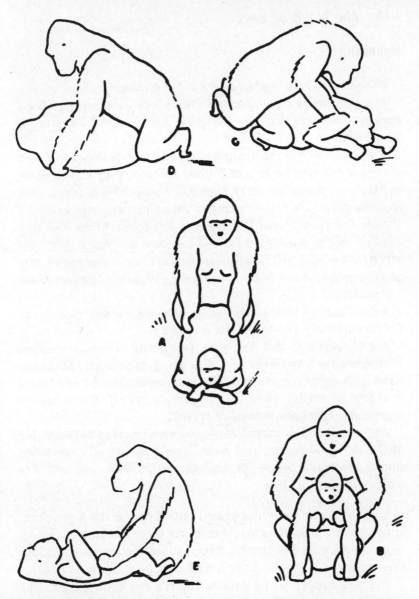

We haven't borrowed these drawings from *Winnie the Pooh*. They are just a few examples of the way gorillas make love, taken from a highly scientific work *The Mountain Gorilla*.

It looks as though the male is the active partner each time. But it's unlikely the female ever gets much of a thrill out of it. One of the positions is reminiscent of the 'missionary position' (*bottom left*).

Spanking

I've got a terrible problem—a kind of madness.

It started when I got spanked when I was quite a big girl. I'd earned it all right, but even though it hurt like hell I enjoyed it very much.

I got such a violent sensation of pleasure both while I was getting it and afterwards that I often went out of my way to make my father and mother angry with me. I succeeded now and then too, and I went on getting spanked until I was about seventeen.

Now I'm twenty, and I've found a boy-friend whom I'm very fond of. We've tried going to bed together too, but I didn't get much fun out of it. All I really wish he would do is give me a really good spanking. A really good walloping—and then be sweet to me afterwards.

I can't get my mother and father to spank me any more—and I'd far rather my boy-friend did it anyway.

But the result is that I'm often very nasty to him. Instead of beating me the way I hope he will he just gets unhappy. He sometimes gets angry too, because I've been unreasonable, and then I love him so terribly much, but he just pushes off. I'm afraid of losing him. I feel so ashamed of myself.

Do you think I'm crazy? Have you ever heard of anybody like me? I'm so desperate, and have been thinking of committing suicide, because I made life hell for my parents, and now I'm making life hell for him.

You're neither batty nor crazy, but of course it's a problem. If you were a little older you'd discover there are long queues of helpful men who'd be terribly happy to let you irritate them and then give you a spanking for it and then be sweet to you.

But you happen to be young, and it's not certain that your young boy-friend will understand you if you explain things to him. He might get scared, and then it would paralyse him completely. We're a little afraid of it. But it's a good thing that you yourself see your problem so clearly.

You ask if we've heard of similar cases before. Lord, yes. We so often hear of men who come home drunk and beat their wives, and the end of it all is sweet reconciliation. The neighbours wonder why the wife stays with the brute, but presumably she feels a little bit the way you do—without realizing it.

In other words we're certain you'll find masses of men who find your idea quite enchanting once they realize its existence.

The problem is to find someone who's mature enough and sensible enough to laugh at it and say, 'Fine, it's okay by me!' If you find a man of this kind, your problem will be greatly reduced.

Another thing: we can't exclude the possibility that your young boy-friend may be mature and sensible. You could try, just carefully, telling him about a girl you know, couldn't you?

i. & s.h.

Beating

My mother used to beat me when I was a child. I think she derived sexual pleasure from it, because she made no attempt to hide the fact that she worked herself up into a sort of ecstasy.

I've never beaten my children and I'm thankful I've never felt the desire to do so. And I'm certainly not the type that thinks it would be wonderful to meet a woman who really enjoys a good spanking.

I beat my wife quite regularly, usually about once a month if we can find an opportunity to be alone. She lets me do it, not because she enjoys it, but to please me.

But once in a while she does actually ask me to keep it up until she has an orgasm. It's usually when she lies on top of me, and I smack her while we're having intercourse.

To me it seems as if she becomes a warmer, more affectionate mistress when she's had a good spanking, and we're always the best of friends afterwards, even though she's been writhing in pain.

However, the pleasure is mainly on my side. I've often asked her if there's anything she'd specially like, any special desire which I could fulfil in return, but she says there isn't.

Do you think I should see a psychiatrist? I'm not at all keen, because I do so enjoy it.

We've printed your letter, despite the fact that we're just about getting smothered in letters about spanking and presume we'll get a lot more. But the interest seems to be very marked.

It's not us, but your wife who can decide whether you ought to get somebody to help you overcome your particular interests. If your wife can have an orgasm in this way it doesn't exactly suggest that it's a very serious problem as far as she is concerned —she might even miss it a bit if you changed your ways?

But it's not very easy to change when the pleasure has been as intense as it apparently has been in your case. In order to effect a change in a person's mentality, a genuine desire must be there —a desire to be changed.

Another reason why we've printed your letter is because all the letters we receive about spanking and the pleasures derived from beating or being beaten come from people who have been beaten when they were children, or during their youth.

Makes you think, doesn't it?

i. & s.h.

Doesn't Like Feeling Sore

I hope you can help me with a problem which is getting terribly on my nerves.

The thing is that my husband is impotent, and yet not impotent. When we get undressed in the evening, and I dance around in my birthday suit, he's quite likely to feel like making love to me, and then he asks me to come to bed with him. But hardly has he got his penis up before it flops down again—before either of us has had an orgasm.

And then comes the worst part. He gives me a spanking and says it's my fault, and then I cry and get afraid of him. I don't like being spanked, even though I've read in your column that there are women who do—and men too. I've tried to see if he gets an orgasm by giving me an undeserved walloping, but he doesn't: in other words there's nothing sexual connected with it.

We're thirty-eight and forty and have no children. If he keeps it up I suppose I'll have to run away from him one day.

As we gather he doesn't normally beat you, there's probably a certain amount of sexual connection. Perhaps, consciously or unconsciously, he himself has a yearning to be beaten. It's not certain—we only mention it as a vague possibility.

One thing is quite clear, namely that he doesn't know enough about how even the most impotent of men can satisfy even the most demanding of women.

We suggest you show him your sensible letter and our attempt to answer and advise.

Then you'll have to discuss the matter with him thoroughly and try to see if you and he together can work out a form of coital technique that at all events gives you some form of satisfaction. This often results in the man's desires returning, so perhaps this alone will solve some of your problems.

But you must also get him to study some of the latest books on sexual relationships and sex technique.

Most people sniff a bit when they hear anything about its being necessary to have any knowledge of 'technique' in connection with sexual intercourse. Of course it isn't necessary if all you want to do is reproduce your kind—the way animals do. But if you permit yourself the luxury of thinking that a woman is at any rate a sort of human being too—then you have to learn the odd thing or two.

i. & s.h.

Thoughtful

The girl who wrote to you not long ago about so badly wanting to be spanked and feeling ashamed about it is neither crazy nor abnormal. Women like her are loving, faithful, honest and affectionate—and they enjoy being made a fuss of.

*But women are much too reserved. Men aren't thought-readers.
So women must state their wishes openly—and then they'll have
them fulfilled all right. It's marvellous.*

I've tried it. It's lovely.

We've had stacks of letters like yours from men who'd be
terribly happy to be of help to women who'd like to be spanked.
We've also had a few from women who like being spanked,
consoling the girl you mention with the fact that it's lovely to
find an understanding man.

Finally, we've had quite a number of letters from men who
long to find a woman who will give them some corporal chastise-
ment. These men have a really bad time, because there don't
seem to be so many women who think it's fun to go whacking
away at a man. But they do exist.

i. & s.h.

Last Spanking

*I read with interest some time ago a letter from the girl who felt
ashamed about wanting to be smacked, and in connection with this
I'd like to ask why can spanking during childhood produce a
yearning for punishment of this kind in adults? And why is it that
girls in particular seem to feel the urge?*

*I was constantly beaten throughout my childhood. When I was
eighteen or nineteen, and my parents wouldn't punish me any
more, because they probably thought I was too old to be beaten,
what I sometimes did was—when I knew I was alone in the house
—I'd stand in front of the big mirror in the bedroom and give
myself the most terrific spanking on my bare bottom with a
hairbrush.*

*When I got married, my husband soon found out the best way
to make me satisfied. I get a thorough spanking from him at
regular intervals, and now and again I have a violent orgasm right
in the middle of it. But we're happy this way, and I hope the girl
who wrote to you will come to an arrangement with her boy-friend
too.*

It's nice when two people can work out things for themselves —without worrying too much. Congratulations!

It's hard to say whether there are more women who feel this sort of urge than men, because it's never been investigated, and women don't even need to realize they've got the urge. All they need do is pick themselves a severe husband and irritate him.

Why is also hard to say, but during puberty most youngsters flare up rather easily, and it's not very far from pain to sexual pleasure.

i. & s.h.

PS. Here we'd like to bring the discussion about spanking to a close. It appears to be something that preoccupies a great many people. We thank the many readers who have written to us on the subject.

Hands Up

We live in a district where there are lots of children. We've got three ourselves, and one of them is a little girl aged four. The other day, when I was hanging up washing, I discovered that she had gone into the bicycle-shed with a little boy. He is five, an only child, and also lives in this district. He'd pulled her trousers down. I scolded them and told my little girl she wasn't to play with that boy any more. Now I don't really know what to do, because I think the neighbours ought to know about it, and that I ought to warn them, but on the other hand I don't like gossip. What would you advise me to do? I would so like to do the right thing.

Yes, we parents easily get scared by this sort of curiosity. We assume the boy has a whole lot of feelings and thoughts which a little chap of his age shouldn't have at all. But strictly speaking it's us grown-ups who have made nakedness so exciting.

If the boy had been told things clearly and been given straight answers to his questions—or if he'd had some sisters whom he'd seen without any clothes on—then he wouldn't have found it so burningly necessary to take such drastic steps with your daughter.

We who are now grown-up have probably all experienced the same sort of thing as your daughter—or have been a little boy who pulled trousers down ourselves.

So there's no reason for panic or earnest deliberation. If you can, you should tell your daughter the story that's got nothing to do with storks—she's old enough to hear it. Do it as honestly and straightforwardly as you can.

But really it hasn't got so much to do with the boy and his inquisitiveness. And there's certainly no cause to forbid your little girl to play with the boy, or to warn others about him.

It may sound a little glib to say this, but we wonder if you wouldn't actually agree with us if we said we hoped that neither boys nor girls will lose the urge to pull each others' trousers down?

i. & s.h.

Exhibitionist

My daughter and I have been embarrassed by a young man who has placed himself in front of us and masturbated.

It's not the first time. Once my husband scolded him for it, but it didn't help, because six months later he did it again. Another time when he did it we all three went over to the window in turns and laughed out loud at him. That helped a bit.

The other day I heard a little girl shout at him: 'When are you going to run round naked again?' And we've heard that he exposes himself in front of children.

What are we to do? I don't like going around with this knowledge, I mean as a grown-up person, without doing something.

Supposing he attacked a little girl!

It's difficult to do the right thing, because society takes these things much too seriously.

But we can reassure you that it's very seldom an exhibitionist attacks anyone.

If he'd been a pretty young girl he'd be able to make a fat living out of it. Without any trouble.

Well now, so he's got this slightly silly but strictly speaking fairly harmless urge. The little girl's remark would also seem to indicate that she takes it very lightly. Children do, you know, until we teach them to be frightened.

It is our civilization that has somehow worked out that the sight of a naked man must have a harmful effect on the eyes and

minds of our girls and women—especially if the said man is in
a really gay and vivacious frame of mind.

Well, this chap doesn't sound all that vivacious. It seems more
as if he's in need of human contact and has therefore started
this rather awkward form of approach. A bit stunted, one might
call it, because in point of fact it doesn't help him to achieve
what he's after, namely to be accepted.

Reporting him to the police won't solve his problem. Then
he'd have to find an even more forced form of satisfying his
urges. He really ought to be treated.

Try talking to the local doctor to see if he can think of something that won't result in scandals, threats and sensation-
mongering but will help the young man and stop him behaving
this way.

i. & s.h.

Exhibitionism?

*You have frequently raised an eyebrow at the term 'modesty',
and you tend to squirm when people claim to be 'bashful'. But
certain things produce a very genuine feeling of bashfulness in
some people—including me. It's the sort of bashfulness that doesn't
get any less pronounced with the years.*

Luckily we can't really count on the feelings we ourselves
believe to be 'genuine', 'inherent' or 'natural'. We say 'luckily'
because the feelings involved are often those which prevent us
from enjoying life—sex life in particular.

We'd prefer to answer you with a fable, a little fairy-tale about
women, bicycles and market analysis. It dates from before the
days of the mini-skirt.

Once upon a time there was a man who wanted to invest quite
a large sum of money in something sensible—something people
really needed. He thought of this and that, and had a look round.

His attention was attracted by the famous hordes of Danish
girls riding bicycles in light summer frocks that flapped up round

their ears in the Danish breezes. He observed—like so many others, but with a particular steady gaze—how they kept on trying to pull their flimsy skirts down over their knees and often very nearly fell off in the process. He saw how motorists collided with one another, and how pedestrians often stepped right out into the road without thinking. And all because of these lovely things that kept on getting exposed against the girls' wishes.

He was a thorough sort of chap, and so first of all he had a little test done. He had a thousand girls interviewed, and it turned out that practically all of them were very much aware of the problem—and that they found it most irritating to have their skirts always blowing up. And in answer to the question 'Would you be interested in a device which would keep your skirts in place?' nine hundred and ninety-nine of them delightedly replied, 'Yes!' (The last girl was actually Swedish, and confessed later that she hadn't understood the question.)

Our cautious friend with all the money then put a few engineers to work on the job. It transpired (after a test conducted in a wind tunnel with stationary bicycles and lengths of organdie pinned on to wax dummies) that two little lumps of lead, each weighing thirty-five grams and attached to the seam at the bottom of the material, were perfectly capable of resisting a wind force of approximately eight or nine yards a second. They could be fixed in position by means of a special zip-fastener.

Production was begun. Thanks to a generous grant from the Ministry of Transport, they managed to keep the price down to threepence a set.

The first production run was of fifty thousand sets of weights, and the brilliance of the idea was lauded in the press and on TV and radio programmes specially devoted to the subject. Not one female cyclist in the whole kingdom of Denmark remained in ignorance of the existence of these new 'skirt-weights'.

After a campaign lasting six months, our friend took stock of the situation. Two pairs had been sold to a clergyman in Jutland who was in the habit of riding to church on a moped.

Who said anything about women's 'natural' bashfulness?

i. & s.h.

7. Homosexuality

Many people think of a homosexual as a namby-pamby fellow who runs round trying to seduce people—or as a masculine, short-haired schoolmarm type.

There are both masculine men and feminine women who, independently, live in 'marriages' with people of their own sex —marriages which are often better and more stable than those of many heterosexuals.

But they have no legal rights. Perhaps one of them gives up his/her job in order to look after their mutual home while the other goes out to work. Suddenly the breadwinner dies—and the 'kept' partner is pitched out into the streets after perhaps many years of marriage. A distant uncle inherits from the deceased and a delighted landlord rubs his hands gleefully at having got rid of the swine.

But it's even worse to live all alone and have a fondness for persons of your own sex.

Different

I am twenty-six, and ever since I was thirteen have realized I was different. In the beginning it wasn't so difficult. I associated with young men, but gradually it dawned on me that I couldn't marry, that in this way I could never be happy, nor could I make another person happy. I could feel revulsion, and that's something you can't hide.

I'm now twenty-six and live alone. I'm hardly ever cheerful, feel unhappy and abnormal, but despite all this I have to go on living the way I am.

Possibly the easiest way out would be to make an end of it all, but it's against my convictions and faith. Have you any advice to give me? I would so like to be normal and live like other people.

When I hear about homosexuals, or people start talking about them, I can hardly eat or sleep for several days on end. At the place where I work, when the conversation drifts round to the subject, they usually talk about 'filth', 'perversion', etc. But have we asked to be like this? Can we help it? If only others would think about it and show a little understanding.

Yes, yours is indeed a cruel fate—one you share with many famous writers. Hans Andersen, for instance, has written a number of beautiful and moving descriptions of what it feels like to be ostracized just because one isn't like the rest.

But there are avenues open to you.

If you make a big, protracted and costly effort—and if you really do want to get rid of your revulsion for the opposite sex, psychoanalysis can help in some cases if you're lucky.

i. & s.h.

What Shall I Do?

I am a man of thirty-two. I've always been moved more by the sight of a beautiful boy than by a girl. This is probably why I don't get much pleasure out of going to bed with girls.

However, homosexual relations fill me with a revulsion that is greater than my passion.

Physically I'm OK, and am therefore pestered by the desire for sexual release at regular intervals—and mentally I long to establish a relationship with another person. I also love children.

Should I give in to my increasing feeling of loneliness and social pressures (which are strong), get married and produce some children?

Perhaps some kind-hearted woman would accept marriage without love on my part—perhaps because she might feel she could convert me. But what will happen in ten years' time? I do so badly want to avoid hurting anybody, on the other hand I can hardly face remaining alone for the rest of my life.

Forgive me for remaining anonymous. My courage failed me.

Anonymous letters are welcome.

Let's just try to assess your situation. You seem to be bi-sexually interested, perhaps with the balance tipping in favour of your own sex, perhaps mainly interested in boys.

We can see various possibilities for you. First of all a young woman of the kind known as 'the boyish type', that is to say with a boyish figure. Another possibility is the homosexual, or woman with lesbian interests who would also like to have children.

Sometimes a good doctor with experience in psychiatric problems can help people like yourself to become more clearly aware of their real wishes. And certain magazines dedicated to the interests of homosexuals can often be of help in realizing such wishes.

i. & s.h.

Men and Women

I'm a man and I'm very fond of women. Still, I never find it revolting to see or hear about two women making love—not nearly as revolting as if I hear about two men lying on a bed slobbering away at each other.

Why?

You probably regard the fact that you don't like the idea of men being in love with each other as a completely natural, instinctive form of revulsion.

But it isn't. It's something society has taught you. We keep banging into young people's heads, in many small ways, the fact that homosexuality is revolting. Particularly amongst men. We're far more tolerant towards women. Girls are allowed to kiss each other and dance with each other, but just you try making advances to another young man at the local village hop. . . . A very clear *fear* of male homosexuality exists.

But there are other countries and other communities that regard these matters in a completely different light, societies in which young men are welcome to walk arm in arm and dance with each other. There are even societies in which it is a young man's duty to place himself at the disposal of other men for sexual purposes—until they marry a woman. And this doesn't turn these young men into fanatical homosexuals. They have children and are fond of their wives.

i. & s.h.

Homosexual?

I myself believe I am a grown-up, mature person of twenty-five. I've tried things with various girls, but without success. Now I'm beginning to have a strong suspicion that I'm homosexual and have just been suppressing it.

I would like to investigate the matter in practice, but am not too keen on doing it in my home town. I'm going off on a trip round Europe late this autumn.

Where can I go in order to find people who feel the way I do—people who may feel the way I do?

I feel very lonely.

You don't say in what way you've experienced fiascos with girls.

You were probably, like all other men (and women) born bi-sexual (as a matter of fact multi-sexual). This means—at least in theory—that you can be stimulated by your own as well as by the opposite sex.

As a rule it is the opposite sex that stimulates us, but experience in prisons, on lonely expeditions, etc. proves there is a certain amount of truth in the old adage: 'If you haven't got what you need, use what you've got.'

Normally, the ability to be stimulated by other men is suppressed so forcibly in the majority of men that they'll swear to you the very idea appals them. It is the pressure exerted by society, society's condemnation of homosexuality, which causes this.

(Society is much more tolerant of female homosexuality. That is why the majority of mature women, if they were completely honest with themselves, would admit that the thought of having sexual relations with another woman would not go entirely against the grain.)

But you would like to try a homosexual experience abroad. A homosexual magazine in Copenhagen has published a 'guide', in which you can find the names and addresses of hotels, bars, public baths and other meeting places for homosexuals in several hundred cities all over the world.

i. & s.h.

Can One be Seduced?

Can one become a homosexual just by having sexual intercourse with a homosexual—if one's inclinations don't happen to lie that way to start with? I've just read a silly book about some male prostitutes—young boys—in which this happened.

You're quite right. Not many people believe in the seduction theory.

But we'll admit there's just a little in it. If a person discovers that sexual satisfaction can also be obtained in the unorthodox manner, well, the possibility is always there. But of course, it's tied up with the fact that none of us—neither you nor ourselves

—was born either heterosexual or homosexual by nature. It's nothing inherent in us, instinctive.

Presumably we are all born capable of obtaining sexual satisfaction with persons of the same sex as well as with the opposite sex. But society tells us it's only nice to do it with persons of the opposite sex. And so most of us are obedient and stick to it, but some of us are barred from it and obliged to turn to the same sex. However, it's quite common for so-called homosexuals to be bi-sexuals, i.e. capable of enjoying sexual intercourse with persons of both sexes.

i. & s.h.

Good Friends

Now and then one hears people talk in a disparaging way about homosexuality. Those who do just can't have tried it.

I'm a young man of twenty and I believe I'm completely normal. Admittedly I haven't got myself engaged yet, but I've often slept with girls and got great pleasure out of it.

I've got a friend who's a bit older than I am. He's a homosexual and my very best friend. I have sexual relations with him once in a while, because it means a great deal to him and I don't find it unpleasant.

Is there anything wrong in our continuing? We've agreed that the day I get engaged our sexual relationship will stop. But we've agreed to carry on being good friends.

You write about your friend and about yourself as if he were greatly attracted by you but you had no feelings for him and just did him a favour now and again.

But the relationship can't be that cool, can it? He seems to be predominantly homosexual, while you can react sexually to both sexes, i.e. behave bi-sexually. We say this because you shouldn't try to kid yourself that your relationship means nothing to you.

You also write that you and he have agreed to stop and just be good friends the day you get engaged to a girl. This is no doubt what you fully intend to do, but you cannot be sure that your friend will feel the same way. He is fond of you and will promise you anything, but this doesn't mean that it will be easy for him to stick to the agreement.

We don't wish to make the decision for you—whether to carry on or not, that is. We believe, like you, that the day you find a girl and fall in love with her, you won't find it hard to stop—but you must count on the fact that it will be hard for your friend.

i. & s.h.

No More Men

I'm a woman of fifty. I have never had an orgasm with a man but only by masturbating. I've tried everything, including hormone injections, but nothing has helped.

Recently I've found myself being attracted by my own sex. I look at pictures of girls in various states of undress and imagine myself going to bed with them.

Is there any sort of a club or the like through which one can get into contact with women who have the same outlook?

We admit that men are sometimes unbelievably clumsy, and it seems you've been unlucky.

We don't think you're homosexual, that you will only be able to have an orgasm with a woman, but we do believe that you have gradually come to give up your faith in men because they've let you down so often. And so you turn, very understandably, to your own sex, and say: 'Women probably know more about what a woman likes.'

This isn't exactly wrong—but what about giving men another chance?

We don't know if you're married, but if you are, try just once more talking to your husband about it frankly and getting him to read some of the latest books on sexual enlightenment—books from which the majority of men can learn quite a lot of things that nobody knows by instinct.

This enlightenment really is necessary to help get rid of a great deal of persistent superstition.

There should be good chances of finding a woman with the same ideas as yourself if you put an advertisement in one of the homosexual magazines. But what about giving men another chance? We know they haven't deserved it—but even so.

i. & s.h.

8. Appearance, plastic surgery and breasts

One of our friends once played a rather unkind game with his friends. Whenever he found himself alone with one he would begin to study him or her in silence, carefully, and for a long time.

It never failed. His victim always ended by exclaiming 'I know I've got fat legs, a big bottom . . .'—or whatever it was that upset the person about his or her appearance. Whereupon our wicked friend would grin and say: 'Well, I just wanted to hear what *your* sore point was!'

We've *all* got our sore points. Most of us learn to live with them, and get on pretty well. It would be awful if we all looked like Brigitte and Marlon.

Do Your Ears Stick Out?
Then Listen!

What is a plastic operation? There are various things I don't like about my appearance. I have got flapping ears.
Who does one apply to?

There are a number of private clinics. As a rule they are very expensive. They are mostly to be found in Germany, France and the USA.

We often get letters like yours, so we had better answer you in full. The term plastic surgery is used to cover operations intended to improve a person's appearance. Ears that stick out can be made to lie flatter against the side of the head, breasts that are too big or too floppy can be made smaller, crooked noses can be straightened, and so on. It's mostly used in the case of accidents in which people have suffered some form of disfigurement. But it's becoming more and more common.

Considering how much some variation in his or her appearance can cause a person mental suffering—far more than the physical pain of appendicitis or a broken limb—it's disgraceful that plastic surgery is not regarded with greater respect. It's not considered 'nice' to be vain about one's appearance, but in point of fact we all are, more or less openly—particularly less.

Unfortunately it's just 'not done' to have some minor defect put right and thereby render life a little less intolerable.

We speak so sentimentally about freckles, and say a little girl 'looks so sweet' when her face is covered with them, and we tell a little boy not to be so silly if he complains about the way his ears stick out. But in point of fact this is just failing to respect another person's feelings.

If a person is really unhappy about his or her appearance it should be an entirely reasonable thing to have something done about it—and by one of the finest surgeons in the country at that. Today it's something you hardly dare talk about. It's not a completely natural thing to go to your doctor and have him pass you on for treatment by a specialist. But there are certain possibilities—and you *can* get help if you show a spot of insistence.

We're not doctors, so we've turned to a colleague, who tells us that flapping ears and deformed noses can in some cases be dealt with at no cost to the patient at all. Flapping ears can be 'pinned back' in less than an hour—more or less 'while you wait'!

i. & s.h.

It Doesn't Grow any Bigger

I'm a young man of twenty-one and I've known lots of girls and it's lovely.

But I've got a little problem, and it's that my penis hasn't grown any bigger for the past five or six years. Can you give me an explanation?

I've heard about hormone pills. Do you think they would help?

Yes, we can give you an explanation. A young man's penis

doesn't grow any bigger after he's reached the age of fifteen to twenty. And it is at this age that a boy/young man is most potent. (So hormone pills won't help.)

Here we're using the word *potent* in the sense that he is able to react sexually at short intervals. As a man gets older these intervals get longer.

But real ability, real potency, has got nothing to do with the size of a man's penis. A skilful and imaginative lover can satisfy a woman in the most wonderful manner—without having to use his penis at all.

Attaching importance to the size of the penis is one great big misunderstanding. Most men admittedly do, but it is the result of ignorance concerning what women really want. Experienced lovers don't worry themselves; they know that no matter whether their penis is large or small, the woman's vagina will adapt itself beautifully.

Inexperienced women, who have just discovered that women don't have orgasms as easily as they had expected, may suffer from the same delusion. It's so easy to believe that if the man's penis had been bigger, an orgasm would have come much more easily. But it's just superstition.

As we have repeatedly pointed out, the focal point of a woman's sexual pleasure is her clitoris—the little button situated just above the entrance to her vagina—and it is constant, direct tickling of this little organ that switches on a woman's orgasm. But it needs more loving attention and coaxing than an ordinary electric switch.

This is why it is seldom enough for a woman just to have a penis hopping up and down inside her vagina, even though there is a connection between the smaller vaginal lips and the skin on the clitoris. In other words, when the smaller vaginal lips are pushed back and forth by the movement of the penis as it glides in and out, an indirect influence is brought to bear on the clitoris—in exactly the same way as the skin on a penis slides backwards and forwards when the scrotum, or testicles, are pulled.

i. & s.h.

None of Your Nonsense!

*What is the normal size of a penis, (a) when hanging limp, and
(b) when erect. I know you've preached endlessly about the fact
that the size of a penis doesn't make any difference, but still, I'd
like to know anyway, as there doesn't seem to be anything in all
the text-books on the subject.*

*My own penis measures 3¾ in. when limp and 5½ in. when it's
at its stiffest, and I think this must be less than most people.
I'm twenty-one.*

Now then, don't try to talk your way round it!

All our talking round things and preaching—call it what you
like—seems to have been in vain seeing that you continue to
be interested in the question. We're afraid you'll have to put up
with our talk anyway, because it's important to make you
understand that you've asked the wrong question.

Your penis doesn't measure 3¾ in. when limp. It was 3¾ in.
long on the occasion—or occasions—when you measured it.
But try going for a bathe in the sea one cool summer's day and
then measure again! Your penis isn't 5½ in. long at its biggest
either, because it only reaches this state just before ejaculation.
At such moments very few people bother to think about tape-
measures.

Finally we must repeat, in our endless fashion, that women
whose husbands have large penises are not necessarily more
satisfied than women whose husbands have smaller penises.

Most women find it difficult to have an orgasm. And so it is
both understandable and excusable—but wrong—if they start
thinking: 'If only he had a larger penis, or a longer penis, or
could keep going longer, everything would be so much better
for me!'

It's understandable—but it's still wrong.

Masters and Johnson mention that they have come across
penises measuring between 2¾ in. and 5¾ in. when limp—
and that they increase between 2 and 3¼ in. when in a state

of sexual excitement. The smaller ones more, the bigger ones less.

We hope you'll excuse us.

i. & s.h.

PS. Let us repeat that a woman's vagina can permit the passage of a child's head, but can also close tightly round a pencil.

The Things One Hears!

I read your column regularly and am surprised to hear about all these naïve men who complain about their penises being too small.

I'm a woman of sixty-five and I've had oceans of experience of men, so I can reassure the worriers they've got nothing to worry about.

Think of it this way. If you've got an itch in your ear, what's the best thing to scratch it with, a matchstick or a clumsy thumb?

Thanks for your letter. We're sure it'll have a more reassuring effect than theoretical talk from us.

A woman's vagina isn't a yawning chasm in which small penises go dashing round in a flat spin. It's more like a collapsed tube—like the inner tube of a bicycle without any air in, if you like—with elastic walls that can close tightly round any size of penis, small or large.

As we have said before, it isn't the size of the penis that brings a woman to orgasm. It's tickling the right place—the clitoris—in the right way.

i. & s.h.

Help!

I hope you can help me, but I don't really think you can. I would so like to get some advice that might save me—and, in particular, somebody else—from something disastrous.

I am a man of forty-two. Twenty-three years ago, when I was nineteen, I went to bed with a girl for the first and only time in my life. She was twenty-five and she was the one who asked me to, and encouraged me. I was terribly unsure of myself and nervous and literally had no idea how to start.

When she discovered I had only a very small penis she looked at it with a sneer and said: 'Heavens, a little thing like that's no use for anything except piddling with!' After which she told me to get out.

Nobody who hasn't experienced the same thing can imagine what sort of a humiliation this was. It's ruined my whole life.

Things have got to such a state now that—well, at certain periods I just can't look at a girl, especially if she's a bit provocative, without feeling the most violent sexual desire and at the same time a black hate and a wish to inflict physical pain.

Unfortunately I can feel this way about very young girls, children that is, as well as grown women. But as yet I haven't dared try to contact any woman. I go round terrified in case I should suddenly find myself attacking a girl—especially, of course, a child.

What can I do? It would be terrible for the girl or the child—and nobody would pity me, for my kind of hell can only be understood by somebody who's in it himself.

We're afraid we can't help you very much, but we believe that a psychiatrist—or a clever psychoanalyst in particular—would be able to help you to get rid of some of the pressure.

If you've been following our column you'll realize that the girl behaved both stupidly and naïvely. The size of a man's penis has nothing to do with a woman's sexual satisfaction, but many women believe it has because women often experience difficulty in having an orgasm at all—quite apart from the size of the penis.

You can still become a better lover than the majority of men with larger penises if you get rid of some of your hate and get to know a mature woman.

i. & s.h.

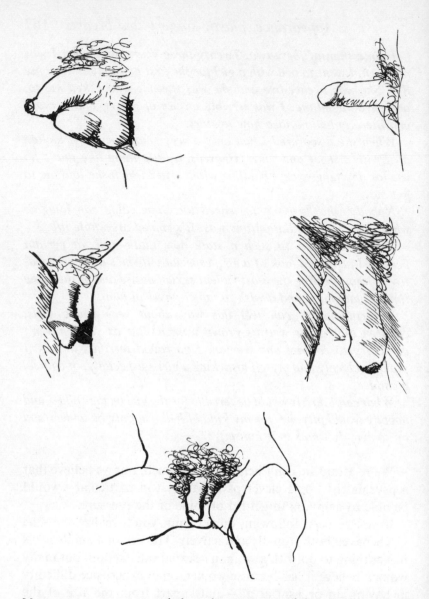

Most men are very concerned about the appearance of their genital organs—length and thickness in particular give rise to many speculations, which ought to be quite unnecessary if only men (and women) would realize that these are not the important factors. Neither from a woman's point of view nor from a man's. Here's a small selection of penes. You won't necessarily find yours among them. They are just examples to show we're all different.

Excerpts from Letters

I've been studying myself in the mirror and I'm convinced there's something the matter with my genital organs. They look very strange!

. . . I'm very fond of women, but you must admit that female genitals aren't exactly beautiful.

May we answer both your letters together, even though you don't know each other?

We're always hearing this sort of thing, and it's practically impossible to make the people who ask these questions understand that they're barking up the wrong tree. Both of you are talking nonsense, fortunately.

We'll try to answer with a fable, a parable. Please think it over!

In the days of ancient Arabia, little boys grew up without ever having seen a woman's mouth. All grown-up women covered the lower part of their faces with a veil. Well, of course little boys had seen little girls' mouths now and then, and very occasionally caught a glimpse of a woman's mouth, but not *properly*.

These little Arab boys grew up into young men full of passionate dreams about women. What really made their imaginations run wild was the thought of the moment when they would be allowed to lift the veil from an adored woman's mouth and then study it and enjoy it properly—caress it and kiss it.

One day, an Arab youth found his dreams had turned into reality. He lifted the veil from his young wife's face and stared in wonderment at her mouth. It was half open and she looked at him bashfully.

'Good God!' he said (or 'Good Allah!' or whatever Arab youths say), 'it looks a bit peculiar!'

His young wife, who'd never seen the lower part of other young women's faces properly either, had often studied her own features privately in the mirror.

'What an ugly mouth I've got!' she'd said to herself. 'I'm sure all other girls have got proper little rosebuds without those ugly teeth and that awful tongue and that revolting fleshy bit that hangs down at the back of my palate. It's going to be terrible when my husband finally sees me without my veil!'

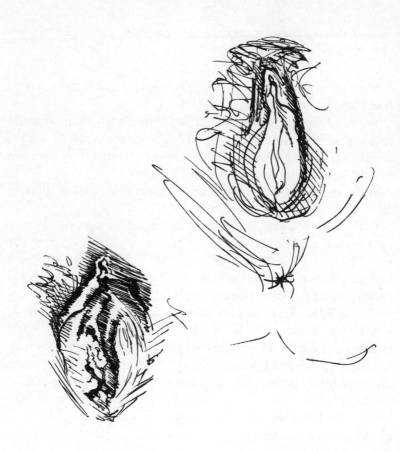

Actually, we would have preferred to have photos of female and male genitals, but for one thing it would have made this book more expensive, and for another there are a number of people who might not be able to take it.

For this particular purpose, drawings are unfortunately not quite accurate enough. We recommend women to have a look at a few pornographic booklets which reproduce colour photos of female genitals.

Of course the comparison has its weak points—like so many parables—because Arab boys had seen lots of men's mouths, and young Arab women probably saw a good many mouths belonging to other young women. And so on.

Even so, we hope you'll see what we're driving at.

i. & s.h.

Pill Problem

After I'd had my first child I began to take contraceptive pills. They've admittedly had the desired effect, but I've also put on weight—about five or six lb—despite the fact that I'm terribly careful about what I eat. And this worries me a lot.

Is there anything one can take to counteract this, or another type of pill that doesn't have this disadvantage? (The pills I take are the ordinary twenty-one-day kind.)

It's true that the Pill often causes women to put on a few pounds, but these few pounds are generally quite decorative. Do you think your worries could be a bit exaggerated?

If you're overweight it's usually a question of a lot of additional weight—in which case five or six pounds extra don't really make much difference.

And if your weight's normal, five or six pounds don't matter either.

i. & s.h.

Breasts

After two births I've lost over twenty-eight pounds and I'm terribly unhappy and self-conscious about the fact that my breasts have gone awfully floppy.

Seeing I'm young and quite a good-looker, it seems terribly unfair to have everything ruined by feeling self-conscious. I'm even self-conscious about it in front of my husband. It's a problem that can spoil lots of love-making.

Who can I go and see about it?

We have the utmost respect for the so-called complexes which many people have because of something to do with their appearance.

But on the other hand we have to face the fact that we can't all go round looking like Marlon and Marilyn. (Lovely Marilyn's breasts were probably quite pendulous too when she relaxed and lowered her arms.)

Our spouses must accept us more or less the way we are, even though that's no reason why we should just let things slide.

Generally speaking our spouses do accept us. It doesn't seem to be any particular problem as far as your husband is concerned. In other words it's something *you* are taking too seriously.

In our experience, practically no woman is completely satisfied with her breasts. Women with small breasts would like to have bigger breasts, and women with big breasts complain about their being floppy. And this despite the fact that a woman's breasts *can't* be big without drooping a bit too.

Well, you're probably heartily sick of all our moralizing by now and would like to have a proper answer. OK. Special surgical beauty clinics exist in various countries. These clinics will usually undertake, for a large fee, to make alterations in a person's appearance.

In some cases, if your doctor recommends it, you can get an operation performed on the Health Service—if he is satisfied that it really *is* a problem.

i. & s.h.

I Wish I Were Fatter

I'm just about ready to give up. I'm nineteen, five foot ten tall, weigh only just under a hundred and twelve pounds and am terribly thin. I think it's silly that people are always telling you how to lose weight, but never about how to put it on. I suppose you'll say 'Go and see a doctor!', but they always give you the same answer: 'Eat more!' But it's not that easy, because I eat as many fattening things as I can and it doesn't help. There must be some special kind of cure. If you can't advise me, can you suggest somebody else?

We don't imagine you want to be fat—just *fatter*, as we've indicated by our heading. There's no reason why you shouldn't weigh thirty pounds or so more than you do.

According to the latest findings, it's not so much fats that fatten as carbohydrates, also known as *sugar* and *starch*, and fats and proteins *in conjunction with* carbohydrates. So if you want to make yourself a little fatter you should eat sweets, bread, sweet things, potatoes, spaghetti and the like—masses— and, generally speaking, take things a bit easier. But talk to your doctor as well!

i. & s.h.

Budding Sophia Loren

Our big girl is now twelve and very angry with us. We have refused to buy her a bra. She's got very small breasts that don't need a bra at all. She says all her friends have got one and that it's we who are unsympathetic and stodgy.

We feel there's time enough to start on that sort of thing when it's really necessary.

This is an unfortunate (in all likelihood not very healthy) fashion among young girls around the age of puberty today. We say 'not very healthy' because we believe that when the connective tissue in the breast is supported it soon becomes weak. Fortunately the trend among the younger generation of grown-up girls now seems to be towards discarding bras altogether.

But your daughter is no doubt right when she claims that 'all the others have got one', so you'll probably lose the battle, and your daughter will be allowed to be what is so terribly important at that age—like the others!

This disease of wanting to be like the others also gives people much older than your daughter sleepless nights.

i. & s.h.

9. The problems of the middle-aged

A young man often feels in the mood for sex, and about the only problem he has with his erection is that it frequently shows—at the wrong moments.

Men are at their liveliest, sexually speaking, between the ages of fifteen and twenty, which is a little impractical, because they generally associate with girls of more or less their own age who seldom ask much more of their sex lives than kissing, cuddling, holding hands and a few deep sighs.

Slowly, laboriously, the young woman develops a slightly greater interest in sex. She often forgets from one time to the next that it can be lovely—and often she and her partner are so ignorant that it isn't lovely at all. In both cases she almost has to start from the beginning each time.

Finally, during her thirties, forties or fifties, she begins to resign herself to the thought of sacrificing herself for her country. Admittedly her husband is no longer quite such a live wire as he used to be in his younger days, but fortunately his interest decreases only very slowly. There is no need for him to worry, but he may have been rejected so many times by his young wife that he fails to notice this more mature woman has begun to get a bit of a gleam in her eye. It's a pity.

In the more fortunate instances, the two of them will have toiled away until they have achieved some satisfactory form of sexual intercourse or other, or some way of making love that gives them both pleasure. But in all too many instances they will have drifted slightly apart from one another on account of disappointments, defeats and fiascos.

Nevertheless, they still dream of achieving simultaneous orgasm with the man's penis inside the woman's vagina—without realizing that it demands deep insight, lots of practice and a great deal of mutual confidence. They cling to various misunderstandings and old superstitions and the man feels himself to be impotent in all sorts of ways. The woman expects the wrong things of him—and then the trouble starts.

Nothing Doing

I'm sixty-two, but don't feel a day older than fifty.

For the past six months or so I haven't been able to get an erection. It doesn't matter what I try in the way of pornographic magazines, books and photos. There's just nothing doing.

We're afraid we've got no tip to offer you, merely the consolation that even younger men can have their ups and downs too. We all have periods in our lives when we feel a little less inclined in this way. It's possible that as we get older the pendulum makes bigger swings and the periods get a little longer.

You don't say whether you're married. Some sort of change of approach in one's marriage can often have a very stimulating effect.

i. & s.h.

PS. Perhaps a massage machine, a vibrator, would do the trick?

Rationed?

You say you don't mind anonymous questions. I'd like to ask one.

My wife will soon be sixty and I'm seventy-five. We've always shared bed and board and both have proper orgasms when we make love. Until recently we used to make love once or twice a week, but a couple of months ago my wife suddenly decided we must be careful not to 'overtax' me.

I work five or six hours a day. My blood pressure and heart have been tested and found satisfactory. I can go for long walks without any difficulty and don't see any need to be careful about 'overtaxing' me. I feel as if I'm being rationed.

I'd like to leave the decision to you and then show my wife your answer.

Will you promise to show your wife the answer in any case? Good! Then let us start by saying that to talk of 'overtaxing' you is nonsense. If we human beings are going to be 'spared' in this respect . . . what's going to be left?

One of our favourite stories is the one about the young and eager female journalist who was supposed to interview a ninety-two-year-old authoress.

'Tell me,' said the young lady, 'when does a woman stop taking an interest in sex?'

'Young woman,' replied the ninety-two-year-old, 'you'll have to ask somebody older than me the answer to that one!'

We're rather afraid (but it's something your wife knows better than we do) that your wife perhaps doesn't have proper orgasms and therefore uses your age as an excuse.

If she blushingly admits that she does have a little trouble in this connection, you must be a man and face up to the confession! And you mustn't use your age as an excuse, for any man, no matter what his age, is capable of satisfying a woman sexually if he takes the trouble to find out how.

i. & s.h.

Not What It Might Be

We're a married couple in our fifties and sixties and get on wonderfully and marvellously together in every way—except in bed.

We believe we've tried everything. Text-books, pornography, kissing and tickling in the right places, which serves to warm me up all right, but doesn't give me an orgasm, because my husband's erection isn't what it might be.

I personally can have an orgasm by myself in no time at all, in fact several violent orgasms in succession, but in the long run it's a rather lonely form of sex life. And it can never produce the same kind of feeling of happiness as it must be to experience the same thing in a man's arms.

I'm strongly tempted to plunge into an extra-marital affair. Give me some advice, if you can!

We can hardly claim to have the right advice for you, the kind that takes every aspect of the matter into consideration. We can only support you in your feeling that you have a right to a completely satisfying sex life.

On the other hand we're rather afraid you may be over-romanticizing the possibilities of an affair with another man. It's probably obvious that strangers will always make more exciting sexual partners than the person you normally spend your days (and nights) with. It goes without saying that the unknown holds out more—and more promising—possibilities than what you already know intimately. An expectation of this kind can often produce an erotic excitement which one's every-day partner cannot compete with.

But in practice, it's seldom that a new escapade can live up to all the expectations—particularly in the case of a woman, because women are more passive and require a greater sense of security in a sexual relationship in order to be able to let themselves go.

We should like to suggest to you that if a woman had to choose between a man who was imaginative and prepared to experiment but had *no* penis (or an ineffectual erection) and a man with a perfect, lasting erection but no imagination, the former would be infinitely preferable.

Most young girls find they have the latter type of man. And most young girls get very little out of sexual intercourse. An erection is seldom the most important thing. So you might find your problems were by no means solved just because you got yourself a man with a powerful erection.

Your claim that you can stimulate yourself sexually much better when you are alone is entirely in accordance with the latest scientific research on the subject. This is bound up with the fact that a woman knows best *where*, *how* and *how hard* she wants to be titillated. Furthermore, a woman is much better able to indulge in the sexual fantasies that are so important to her when there's nothing (and nobody) else to distract her.

It is possible, as we have suggested, that you entertain slightly exaggerated ideas as to how other women normally get on. Perhaps you are searching for a kind of happiness that simply does not exist. But it's obvious that you could and should be able to get on better with your husband.

As you will have seen from other questions and answers in this column, the craze nowadays is for massage machines, vibrators—and with good reason. (See Chapter 11 of this book, *Consumer Guide.*) Perhaps this would be the answer to your problem too?

We are thinking of a letter we had from a woman who described to us how she got her first orgasm with the help of a vibrator and her husband's finger inside her vagina. Then they both enjoyed themselves with the machine and sometimes she managed to have several orgasms. Before discovering this technique she'd had a much more difficult time of it than you describe in your case.

Do you think you could be confusing two things? On the one hand, the feeling (which often coincides with the change of life) that romance is slipping away from you—and on the other, the dream of achieving simultaneous orgasm with a penis inside your vagina.

We can't say. We can only draw your attention to a few possibilities.

i. & s.h.

Think of England!

For seventeen years—from 1930—I was married to a completely frigid woman. (Yes, I know you don't think frigid women exist, and of course you're right, but just listen to what I have to tell you.)

During those seventeen years, not once did she undress in our bedroom. *She always used to wriggle out of her dress and into her nightie (the long-sleeved kind) and then dash out into the bathroom and lock the door before divesting herself of the rest. Then she'd come back, and when we were in bed she'd say in a cold voice: 'You'd better get it over!' It was frightful!*

Then we got divorced, and people said: 'How dreadful of him! Fancy leaving a nice wife like that!'

She got half my fortune and alimony. In point of fact I was the one who should have been awarded damages.

That's what most girls were like in those days—those who are now the mothers of young people today. The old-fashioned way of bringing up children in ignorance and filling them with revulsion for anything concerned with sex.

If I came into the bathroom without any clothes on, this ex-wife of mine used to say: 'How vulgar of you!' One could easily go without sex, she felt. It was just a question of 'strength of character'. And my wife's mother was the sort of woman who would say to her daughter just before her wedding: 'Lie down, close your eyes and think of England!' I'm not saying she did, just that she might well have done.

Holy simplicity!

Now I'm married to a woman who is fifteen years my junior, and fortunately she thinks that the wilder things get within one's own four walls the better.

I thought I'd just tell you a little about the background of suppression, misrepresentation and hypocrisy that has ruined so many marriages.

Thank you for your letter. We think it speaks for itself.

i. & s.h.

Out of Practice

I've been a widower for four years, and now I've met a sweet and lovely woman aged fifty. I myself am fifty-nine.

But even though I've been to see two doctors, both of whom have given me hormone injections and hormone pills, I still can't get an erection. It said 'one pill per evening or night' on the bottle, but even when I've taken three it hasn't helped. I'm very unhappy about it—for her sake too.

You've probably got a bit out of practice. And then you meet a sweet woman and get nervous, wondering if you'll be able to 'manage'. And then you find you can't.

The next time you're even more nervous, and by then the ball has started rolling and the vicious circle has started.

You're unhappy about it—for her sake too.

But this is where the solution lies! Because you can give a woman sexual satisfaction of the loveliest kind without using your sexual organs at all. It's an old superstition—and unfortunately one that's very hard to stamp out—that a woman is just as delighted with a penis as a man is. You can use your fingers, your tongue, anything you like. We've just heard that an electric vibrator has been advertised along with the information: 'Recommended by psychologists'!

Once you've discovered that in point of fact you *are* potent—that you *can* satisfy a woman sexually, because *potent* really means *capable*—then your erection is bound to come back again.

Unfortunately, far too many men cling (so to speak) to their penis (which isn't really *that* important) and think they're *not capable any more*, think they're impotent, just because their penis won't do what's expected of it.

And then nervousness sets in—and that's when the trouble starts.

i. & s.h.

PS. Unfortunately, all too many women fall victim to the same superstition and convince themselves that everything is hopeless. On the contrary! Sometimes it is precisely in this way that women experience sexual satisfaction with a man for the first time.

An entirely different thing is the superstition you hear so often to the effect that a man has just so many rounds of ammunition in his old gun, and when they're expended, well, that's that. In other words, that a man is supposed to be capable of having only so many ejaculations in the course of a lifetime and no more.

Utter rubbish!

(We've never heard the same superstition in connection with women's orgasms, but if any woman should be wandering round with the same belief—that only a certain number of orgasms are allotted to each woman—we would like to reassure her that *that* is complete nonsense too.)

On the contrary:

The same thing applies to one's sex life as to a muscle. If one uses it frequently (and most of us can easily do so), it gets stronger and becomes better and better and reacts more powerfully. This applies to both men and women.

If a muscle is not used it degenerates and has to be trained again.

In other words:

A person's sex life, just like a muscle, improves with use.

A person's sex life degenerates if it isn't used.

'Using a sex life' means getting to the point of sexual excitement and orgasm. Whether this is achieved through masturbation or intercourse with another person is immaterial—from the point of view of training.

The fact that intercourse with another person is more enjoyable than masturbation doesn't mean to say that masturbation is sinful. A full-blown meal at a restaurant with the girl of your dreams (preferably your wife) is likewise more enjoyable than a couple of pork pies at a cafeteria.

But this doesn't mean that either masturbation or eating pork pies is sinful or harmful.

No Fire

Sexual relations are very important in everybody's life, but we're a couple of old crones in our sixties and we've missed the

boat. *We've never been told anything, and we've only just begun
to realize how ignorant we've been.*

*We knew nothing about the clitoris, for instance. But I've got
a wonderful husband, who will do anything for me, and so bit by
bit we've been experimenting with fingers, tongue and an electrical
vibrator which my husband brought home one day. Can you do
yourself any harm with these things?*

*Admittedly I get more out of sleeping with my husband now than
ever before, but still not enough. He always has an orgasm, but I
never do. Well, I've got an appliance in the kitchen which is very
troublesome, but it has given me a little sort of flash, but I won't
say of what—oh dearie me no, I'd feel ashamed of myself. If you've
never had an orgasm when you were young I don't suppose the
chances are very great. Those who have lots of them when young
have fewer as they get older, don't they?*

*Over thirty years ago I went to see our doctor because we
thought I was frigid. She said: 'There can never be any sort of life
in an abdomen like yours!' After that I crept right down under my
eiderdown and cried, because there was obviously nothing I could
do about it.*

*But now, silly old woman that I am, I've gone and got very fond
of my husband (don't laugh at me), and I feel as if I've been
cheated. I'm sorry for my husband's sake that I've been such a
wet rag, but even if I haven't shown much fire, we've had a lovely
time together all the same.*

You sound like a real live wire! And perhaps 'a real live wire'
is just about what that abdomen of yours needs! You deserve
it—so don't give up!'

It's not too late. Kinsey mentions a woman of sixty who was
able to have lots of marvellous orgasms within the course of half
an hour. And this was a woman who had had *no* feelings during
intercourse with a man before she was forty. In many ways she
was a special case, but it shows you can start late and still
outdistance all the rest.

You are understandably impatient. This is a good thing and
yet at the same time not so good. Not so good, because it may

cause you to give up. Good, because it can provide you with the
energy to keep on trying.

You and your husband must find a path that hasn't been used
much before. It will take time, like all forms of path-finding.

So you're not a hopeless old frump, nor a silly old woman
either—and it's marvellous that you should have become even
fonder of your husband, and that you're willing to experiment.

A massage machine is usually an excellent thing provided it
is used on the clitoris and the area surrounding it—and preferably guided by yourself, because you know yourself best, and
can best tell where, and how hard and how much.

And you certainly mustn't feel ashamed of the kitchen appliance you've derived some pleasure from. On the contrary, it's a
kind of entrance ticket, an opening, a touch of something lovely,
something that can be even lovelier. So by all means use it, alone
or with your husband—whatever you feel like. In the long run
you'll *both* derive pleasure from it.

The doctor who said that to you certainly was a fool. In those
days doctors knew *nothing* about people's sex lives. Things are
a little better now. We know of several cases of women who've
only just managed to make a start at your age—and they've
found it gets better and better every six months or so. And it
goes on getting better. Fortunately, sex is something you never
stop learning about—you can never say: 'Well, now I know how
to do *that*!'

Don't think you may be doing anything wrong—and stop
feeling ashamed of yourself! Of course it's easier said than done,
but put in as much practice as you can!

i. & s.h.

One, Two, Three—Bang!

*My husband is in his sixties, and I'm ten years younger. We've
only been married a year, and we've both been married before.*

*By and large we get on very well together, except in bed. My
husband was brought up in the country and wasn't even allowed to
see his little sisters when they were in their underwear. And the*

result is he's still so shy he won't let me see him without any clothes on.

When we get into bed together, we're always in our night-clothes, and he never tries to get me warmed up a bit first but gets cracking straight away. He's keen enough all right, twice a week and no mistake, but it's all over within a few minutes, and so I'm beginning to find it rather uninteresting.

It upsets me so much that I find myself getting into bad moods, one worse than the next, but it's impossible to get him to talk about it. I've advised him to read your books or something else on the subject, but he thinks all that sort of thing is perverse.

He reads your column, so maybe your answer can save our otherwise so harmonious marriage.

Thanks for the confidence you display in us, but the chances of getting him to come round are probably rather small. We think you're completely right.

We'd like to state, as positively as we can, that the majority of men don't know enough about women. Just bouncing up and down isn't enough—no matter how long you keep it up. Most women *are* a little slower at getting off the mark than most men. This isn't anybody's fault, just an unfair fact.

It means, first of all, that a man must study how a woman feels about these things—in particular, of course, the woman he is living with. Secondly, he must understand that no super-human powers of endurance are required of him, no feats of strength—but some imagination and willingness to experiment.

We're very much afraid that fairly tough measures may be necessary to rouse him—perhaps a shock, like your leaving him for instance. It's not a very pleasant weapon, but unfortunately we've seen a great many cases in which nothing less would work. And it's often effective.

Yes, his excuse that he was brought up in a very prudish home is legitimate enough in its way. And he obviously has no incentive to change his ways. He's enjoying himself very nicely as it is.

i. & s.h.

Should We Give Up?

We're an elderly couple of fifty-eight and have been married for thirty-five years. We've always been fond of each other and still are.

I've always been satisfied with our sexual relationship, and we've always assumed that my wife was frigid. We came to the conclusion that this just happened to be our lot.

Now, reading your column, we've learnt a great deal about the clitoris and how important it is. And my wife seems to get more out of it when we sleep together now. She's also become less reserved—but her clitoris seems to be dead. Are we too old?

It upsets her. She feels as if she's been cheated.

Please answer us quite honestly and tell me if there's anything I should do to make things better for her. Do hormones help—and can they be bought without a prescription?

We're very, very happy to have had your letter because it's so encouraging to see that you haven't given up, but take action and persevere and write letters and are impatient.

These are all very good and encouraging signs.

You're not an 'elderly' couple, and you're by no means too old. You're a wide-awake couple and you've got a great many years of love-making ahead of you.

Just get started and keep it up! You'll succeed all right, but it takes time, and you must be prepared to find every little step in the right direction being followed by fiascos and finding yourself 'back where you started'.

(Please see our *Consumer Guide*.)

Perhaps you know, from having seen the same thing in children, that all forms of development take place in jerks? That children suddenly get some illness, and seem two years younger, and then, when they're well again, turn out to have grown older, more mature, all at once, in one big hop?

A woman's sexual development follows much the same pattern. And that's what we forget!

Hormones may help a little, but can only be obtained with a

doctor's prescription. But try that too! Not that hormones are the most important thing.

The main thing is that you and your wife have discovered the great importance of the clitoris if a woman is to get anything out of sexual relationships—which don't *have* to take the traditional form of sexual intercourse.

For instance, it is very important for the woman to be thoroughly 'warmed up' before the man goes into action in earnest, in other words for her to have been thoroughly stimulated and, as a result of this, sexually excited—in fact, for preference, have *had* her orgasm.

Women are by no means as ready for sex at a moment's notice as most men are.

'Be Prepared' is the Boy Scout motto. But it's *much* more important to make sure that a woman is prepared.

Furthermore, we may add that the clitoris is hardly ever titillated sufficiently by the mere fact of the penis sliding backwards and forwards in the vagina—by which time it's usually too late anyway. It's better, in fact best, if the woman has had her orgasm *before* the man starts putting his penis into her vagina. When one has become very, very skilful it is possible, in rare cases, to achieve simultaneous orgasm, but it's by no means common.

In the case of some couples, the man or the woman stimulates the clitoris with a finger, or the man uses his tongue. Others have discovered that an ordinary massage machine—which, please note, the woman should be allowed to handle herself—can be a splendid help.

We haven't the space here to tell you about all the fanciful things human beings have thought up together. We can only give you a little inspiration, and stress that it's equally important to talk matters over before—DURING—and after the act itself.

It's important for the man to be able to listen without feeling his vanity is being hurt—or his prudishness, if he happens to be that way inclined—and for the woman to be able to give orders —instead of giving UP.

i. & s.h.

Pleasure With Others

I'm a man of fifty-six who isn't capable of satisfying his wife because she's very demanding.

My wife is fifty and strangely enough has never been as sexy as she is now. She gets an orgasm several times every time, as a rule five or six times, in fact sometimes eight or nine times in succession. Is it usual? Or can it be due to the fact that she's passed the change of life?

I've told her quite plainly she can do what she likes. And during the last couple of years she's found pleasure in other men. We're fond of each other, and I believe this is my best way of keeping her.

She's got a couple of regular lovers and has sexual intercourse a couple of times a week. It's made her as happy and lively as a twenty-year-old. She says herself she's happy to be able to enjoy life.

I benefit from all this too. Is it wrong of me to let her? Is it wrong of her to do it?

Give me a straight answer and I'll do as you say.

We think you've arranged matters in an admirably sensible and tolerant way. We can only express our whole-hearted approval.

It's by no means unusual for women to become more passionate, skilful and demanding with the years—and to have more orgasms.

The Americans Masters and Johnson were the first to describe, in their report, something that had never been observed and described before in sex literature—the fact that women can be titillated again, just after they've had their first orgasm, and again after the second one—and that the second or third as a rule is the best.

This is something very few men realize, because they judge by themselves. Just after a man has had an ejaculation, i.e. an orgasm, he is totally insensitive to titillation—in fact as a rule it actually hurts if stimulation is continued.

i. & s.h.

'Shun! Stand Easy!

Help a man in despair!

I've read everything you've written about the fact that it doesn't matter whether a man's penis is big or small, whether it's stiff or floppy, and to a certain extent I'll admit you're right.

And my wife is perfectly capable of having an orgasm without a penis inside her vagina—provided I get going with my tongue.

But when she's had her orgasm, and it's my turn, I find I haven't got much of an erection. And you'll admit it's quite a nice thing for me to have, isn't it?

My wife thinks everything is all right. Have you any good advice? I've no idea what the cause can be, and I'm not that young any more.

Well, we must bow to your arguments—or rather, be guided accordingly.

Our suggestion: tie a silk ribbon (or the like) round the root of the penis, i.e. as far up as possible—just tight enough to be comfortable. Make a tight bow-knot—*but so's you can get it off again!*

The point is that the penis swells because the spongy or cavernous tissue becomes filled with blood. This blood runs into the penis through the middle (if we imagine a cross-section), but runs away from it again just under the outer surface. We've tried to illustrate this schematically on the next page.

So if something is tied round the root of the penis, the blood can still run into it and fill it and make it bigger and stiffer, but it can't run away again.

We will add the same advice as we've read in a serious German instruction manual, namely that best results are obtained if the female partner fixes the bow.

(By the way, we should mention that we've had many letters to the effect that these electric vibrators which give pleasure to so many women are also excellent for producing an erection in a man. Perhaps most men would prefer a more powerful massage rhythm, so an apparatus on which the speed can be

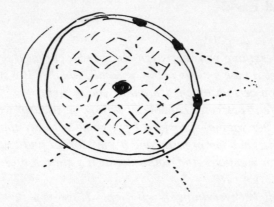

The blood
runs *forward*
here

The blood runs *back* here   Cavernous tissue

In this drawing we've barbarically chopped a penis in half to show how the blood runs *into* the penis through the middle, and *away* again through veins lying just under the skin. This means it is easier to stop the flow away from the penis than the flow into it—and thus help the penis to stay firm.

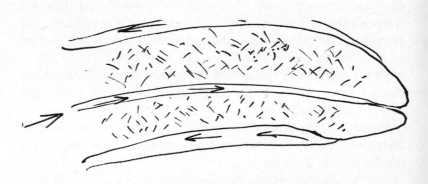

Here the penis has been cut in half lengthwise. The drawing is *very* schematic, but the idea is to show the same thing: the blood runs into the penis through the middle, passes out into the cavernous tissue, and away again through veins just under the surface of the skin.

regulated, or even one with various speeds, would perhaps be preferable.)

Others prefer an elastic band.

An ingenious Copenhagener has told us about his own experiments with a steel ring that can be opened and then

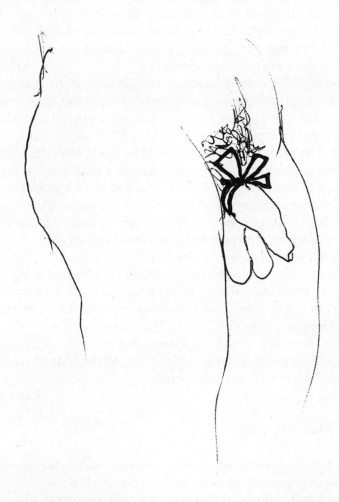

Even if it doesn't work the way it's supposed to, this bow can just be good to look at.

screwed on until it fits. We haven't had an opportunity of trying out this invention yet, but it doesn't sound entirely crazy.

The vital thing is that, first, the blood must be suitably prevented from draining away.

Secondly, what you put on should be reasonably comfortable for the wearer. (It's also possible that women of the kind that are easily provoked to laughter and suffer from penis-envy may find the mere sight enough to put them completely off their stroke. Perhaps this is a good way of finding out whether one has got hold of the right woman?)

Thirdly, the most important thing of all is to make sure whatever you use *can be got off again!* There have been cases in which men, out of sheer playfulness, have pressed their wedding rings on to their penis—just down over the head, or glans, of the penis. The penis then swells up and the blood can't drain away. It's not a good idea. If this happens you simply can't get the ring off at all. It has to be *sawn* off—and it isn't very funny.

There is no danger involved in tying up a penis in the way we have described for a limited period, say up to a few hours. But it shouldn't be allowed to stay on for several days.

So it's very important to be aware of the fact that the penis swells up quite a lot, and that a ribbon may end up being quite tight. In some cases it may be necessary to cut it, in which case it's as well not to have used anything too thin. There should be something to get hold of.

The advantage of a silk ribbon is that it's smooth and there-fore undoes easily when you tug at one of the ends of the bow.

Apart from which it's decorative.

i. & s.h.

I've Shot My Bolt

I'm seventy-seven and my wife is seventy-three. We were both completely ignorant when we got married in 1920.

My wife's attitude at that time was that everything to do with sex was dirty and could just be tolerated in a marriage but no more. I didn't meet with much understanding, as you might say.

Well, we've fumbled along, without knowing that such a thing as a clitoris even existed, or that any preliminaries were necessary. It was always coitus interruptus, because she was always afraid of getting pregnant. Things didn't get any better when she also began to complain she didn't get anything out of it.

It wasn't till after she'd had her change of life, in other words after many, many years of marriage and after our silver wedding, when it wasn't necessary to be careful any more, that a spot of harmony begun to come into our relationship.

Now we've had about ten good years, but during the last few years I've been impotent. Even so, we can still give each other orgasms now and again by petting.

Well, that was just a little about my own background and why I'm writing. I haven't really got any problems. I've shot my bolt.

I do just so badly hope that young people manage to get hold of as much concrete information as possible these days. I can't help thinking how very much different and better everything would have been if fifty years ago I had known all the things you tell young people today.

First, we'd like to thank you for a good letter. Next, we'd like to mention that 'potency', in the old-fashioned sense of the word, is nothing to do with a large or a small penis.

When you say in your letter that you're 'impotent', it's in the old-fashioned sense. Because if you and your wife can give each other orgasms by petting, you are perfectly *capable*, in the sexual sense; in other words potent after all.

You haven't 'shot your bolt'—on the contrary, you should be able to carry on having sexual relations with your wife, and deriving mutual enjoyment from it, to the end of your days.

i. & s.h.

10. The problems of the young

Dear Inge and Sten,
I'm a young man of seventeen. I was going steady with a girl when she insisted on having her way with me. She got it, but her interest in me immediately cooled off. So here I am, left with a feeling of shame, but at the same time wiser. The next time I'll be more firm.

Dear Inge and Sten,
I've just got to know a girl who thinks I'm innocent. I'm so afraid she's going to discover the truth!

We never get letters like these! It's quite thought-provoking, because after all it stresses some of the points on which men and women differ. But is there any cause to cheer on account of *that* little difference?

Simulation

I've never had an orgasm during sexual intercourse. Does it mean there's something the matter with me?
My husband and I have been married for a year and we've got a baby aged eight months. He's twenty and I'm nineteen.
My husband doesn't know I don't get anything out of it, because I pretend I do. Can a man tell if a woman's really had an orgasm or if she's only pretending? He's been so strange recently.
We're both interested all right, and each time I keep hoping something's going to happen. How can I make my breasts firmer?

You're not the slightest bit hopeless. But neither you nor your husband knows enough about what is normal.
Most young women think, as you do, that when you go to

bed with a man you just lean back and spread your legs wide, and then he bounces away, up and down, and then along comes the most marvellous orgasm, all by itself. But it doesn't.

And you've made the same big mistake as so many other girls. You've believed that you must be the one who's abnormal, and then you've resorted to the old solution: you've pretended to be having an orgasm.

But you and he are never going to work things out that way!

If you and he had been married for many years, we would have advised you not to tell him. We would have advised you to tell him you were finding it more and more difficult to have an orgasm, and in this way guide him along the right path.

But seeing you and he have only been married such a short time, we believe your love will be strong enough to stand up to it if you take him into your confidence. Show him your letter and our answer and tell him you are showing your confidence in him by telling him the truth. Tell him men are a lot of vain brutes, and he may get a bit stuffy about it at first, but that you really wanted to please him by telling him about your problems because you thought he'd been unlucky and got himself a difficult wife.

Now you know you're neither frigid nor abnormal nor particularly difficult, and that other girls of your age have precisely the same disappointments and fits of depression.

We repeat: you're completely normal. There's no reason to feel hopeless if you'll just read and try to understand what we're going to tell you now.

All women find it harder to have an orgasm than all men. We can say the same thing in another way. The majority of women don't manage to have an orgasm as quickly and easily as most men do. But because women don't know much about other women's sex lives they think they ought to react just as quickly and easily as men. And because so many women pretend to be having an orgasm, men believe that women can have orgasms just as quickly and easily as they can themselves.

A man manages to have an orgasm by putting his penis up inside a woman's vagina. Men think this is wonderful—and deduce from this that a woman must be just as delighted to feel a penis inside her vagina. But a woman doesn't feel so very much inside her actual vagina. It's not the place where a woman gets her orgasm.

A woman's most sensitive place is just above the entrance to the vagina. It's a little button called the clitoris, the king, the canoeman and a few other pet names. Because it's very much of a favourite spot.

There are a few women who find the sensation of a penis inside the vagina is sufficient stimulation, because the smaller vaginal lips, or *labia minora* as they're known medically, get rubbed backwards and forwards, and as these small lips are connected to the clitoris, the skin on the clitoris that is, this skin is made to glide backwards and forwards too, just like the skin on a penis—and it feels lovely and exciting. But as a rule it isn't enough.

The majority of women, especially young women, need proper, skilful, constant and direct titillation of the clitoris itself—or of the area just round the clitoris. (Especially just before orgasm it's the region just *round* the clitoris and not the clitoris itself that needs tickling. The clitoris itself more or less backs out of the game just before orgasm.)

It may be the woman herself who tickles this area and her clitoris just *before* intercourse proper, or *during* intercourse, for she is the more skilful at it and knows best how she wants it done —or it may be the man, under her expert guidance. (Men, naturally enough, are rather clumsy—and things aren't made any easier by the fact that many women are too shy to say how they want it. In particular, they forget to say when it's nice.) The woman can tickle her clitoris with her own fingers, or the man can use his fingers. It's not unusual for the tongue to be used either—for the man to use his tongue, that is.

You may be a little surprised or scared by these detailed bits of advice, but in our experience women are more robust and sensible in this connection than men.

So perhaps you should prepare your husband rather gently? Men are more sensitive and touchy—and much vainer than women. Far too many men are over-confident, and think a knowledge of sexual relations is something you're born with. It isn't. It's possible that a knowledge of how to reproduce our own kind comes naturally to all of us.

The purely animal process of procreation is something all living creatures manage to achieve without instruction of any form. But one of the things that raises human beings above all the other animal species is precisely the fact that man is capable of developing his sex life into a fine art—not just an animal-like mating dance with the object of reproducing his own kind.

We've answered you at some length because millions of women have precisely the same problems as you—or have had them. Millions of women could have written the same letter to us as you wrote—and millions of women could have benefited from the answer you have now been given. At all events it should save you years of uncertainty and experimenting.

Don't run away with the idea that you have now been told everything and that you now understand everything. You haven't, because it would require even more space—and you don't, because it takes time.

We hope you're mature enough, and sensible enough—and your husband too—to start exploring with him now. Both in theory and in practice. Get yourselves some of the latest books on sex education!

i. & s.h.

PS. Only a very experienced man can tell if a woman is simulating—and taking the Pill may sometimes make a woman's breasts a little firmer.

To the Point

Can a woman have a baby without having had an orgasm during intercourse?

Yes, easily, and unfortunately there are a great many who do. The idea that if a woman remains cold and unresponsive during intercourse she won't become pregnant is just an old superstition. And an old lie. It seems that Providence arranged things a little unfairly seeing that men can't sire children without getting pleasure out of it, while women can have vanloads of children without feeling a thing.

In a manner of speaking, that is.

i. & s.h.

Clitoris

Where is the clitoris? Inside the vagina or between the vaginal lips? My boy-friend says it's inside the vagina. He's been to bed with several girls who've had orgasms.

He tries to make me excited by putting his fingers inside my vagina, but I don't feel anything. But if even virgins can masturbate, surely the clitoris must be outside the vagina?

Personally I've never had an orgasm, so I wouldn't know.

Can a girl who's been to bed with somebody, in other words isn't a virgin, but has never had an orgasm, have an orgasm with someone she's never been to bed with before?

Or does it take a long time to get to know each other's sexual habits? Please excuse my silly questions.

Your questions are extremely sensible. We too have certainly had to ask and study to find things out. Curiosity is the way to knowledge and other pleasures.

So now then. The clitoris is situated between the vaginal lips just above the entrance to the vagina. In other words you're right.

(The skin on the clitoris is joined to the smaller vaginal lips, so when these are rubbed—for instance by the action of the penis sliding in and out—an indirect tickling of the sensitive clitoris takes place, in the same way that if a man's scrotum is pulled, the skin on his penis will slide back and forth. But rubbing in this way is seldom sufficient to produce an orgasm.)

Your boy-friend sounds to be a little young and naïve. It is very, very seldom that a woman has an orgasm the first time she sleeps with a particular man—even if she isn't a virgin—unless the man is very knowledgeable, imaginative and skilful. And even then it's by no means common.

Even when circumstances are favourable, it can take periods of six months or so to get to know each other's ways—and to develop confidence in each other.

i. & s.h.

Ignorant

I'm a boy of sixteen, and for a long time I've been wondering about a few things in connection with going to bed with a girl for the first time.

Does what is generally known as your jock-string break the first time you have sexual intercourse? Does it have to break at all? And if it does, does it hurt very much?

Are you supposed to pull back your foreskin before you have sexual intercourse? Or does it slide back by itself? Don't you have to pull it back if you use a french letter?

I'd be very much obliged to you if you'd answer these questions, because I find them very important and difficult. Otherwise send me a reply in some discreet way, because I wouldn't want my parents to get hold of this letter.

You didn't supply us with your name and address, nor a stamped addressed envelope, so we weren't able to comply with your wishes, but here are the answers.

We don't know the expression 'jock-string', but we assume it's the 'string' of skin that connects the foreskin to the tip of the penis. It is correct that in very, very rare cases it can break if the man goes about things in a very, very violent fashion. We're sure it must hurt, but although the penis is a very sensitive organ, it is not so responsive to pain, heat and cold as to pressure.

Before rolling on a french letter or condom it is best to pull back the foreskin so that there's room for the penis to move. If you use some other method there's no need to think about this problem because the foreskin slides back by itself.

Some men have a problem in that the foreskin is too tight to be pulled right back over the head of the penis, or glans, i.e. the 'knob' at the end that looks rather like a reddish-blue plum. They should practise, i.e. get into the habit of drawing the foreskin back as far as it will go—without actually hurting—so as to stretch it.

i. & s.h.

Phimosis

I can't pull my foreskin back. At any rate I can only just get it back over the tip of my penis. It hurts—and then it's very difficult to push it forward again. What is circumcision?
What shall I do?

Many men have the same difficulty. As a rule the foreskin stretches a bit with the years—especially if you 'train' it. Get into the habit of pulling your foreskin back as much as you can every time you go to the lavatory. (It can actually be quite a jolly form of amusement.)

If it's very troublesome you can go to see your doctor, who may then pass you on to a specialist who can decide whether to perform just a very small operation. As you know, the foreskin isn't very sensitive. It can be rubbed and pinched quite hard without hurting.

Circumcision means cutting off the foremost part of the foreskin. The foreskin is a double piece of skin. If it's pulled out a bit and a small piece is cut off, the severed edges can grow together again, and the result is a *shorter* foreskin that allows the tip of the penis to protrude—and a *wider* foreskin that doesn't press so tightly. As you probably know, most Jews (and millions of non-Jews) are circumcized. It's quite practical when it comes to cleaning all the little nooks and crannies, and the risk of the foreskin getting painfully stuck behind the head of the penis is avoided. But being circumcized doesn't make a man a better lover, which is what some people believe.

s.h.

Too Young for Sex

If I said how old I was you'd think I was crazy writing to you.

You see, I'm much too young for sex and that sort of thing, but I'm very interested. So I'd be grateful if you would answer the following questions.

How old should a girl be before she goes to bed with a boy who uses a french letter? I mean, what's the earliest?

And how old should she be before she goes to bed with a boy who doesn't use a french letter?

What's the earliest age at which a girl should kiss a boy?

Is it normal for one breast to be bigger than the other?

What's the earliest age at which you can start having your periods?

Is it normal to feel shy about talking to one's mother and father?

It would be so easy for us to get round your questions by answering:

It's too early if you yourself say: 'I'm much too young for sex.' We won't say that—but it would actually be a sensible answer.

It's dangerous to drive a car. So one has to know something about cars and traffic regulations before one is allowed to drive. One can have babies without meaning to and contract venereal diseases by going to bed with people if one doesn't know a few things about sexual relations and stick to a few rules.

So it's not so much a question of age, even though in some cases a sense of responsibility comes with age. In other words it is possible to imagine cases of thirty-year-olds and even forty-year-olds who don't know enough, don't stick to the rules and haven't got a sufficiently developed sense of responsibility—and so, strictly speaking, shouldn't indulge in sex.

When you ask, 'How old should one be?' we have to answer evasively and say: 'One should possess knowledge and a sense of responsibility.' And even then we're being a little bit sanctimonious, for many adults and married people don't have sufficient knowledge and aren't sufficiently responsible, even if they have been given the blessings of the Church or the local registry office and told they can go ahead and have sexual relations with each other.

A condom, or french letter, isn't the best form of birth control, but is probably the method many young people find easiest to use.

In some countries there are millions of people who have got married at the age of twelve or so and had children, but this doesn't mean they were more developed or more knowledgeable and responsible than the twelve-year-olds of this country.

So you see, your questions aren't easy to answer. The easiest thing is for us to moralize and say 'Wait as long as possible!' and 'Don't!' But youngsters don't listen to this sort of thing anyway.

You will also understand that unless you use a french letter— or some other method of contraception—you shouldn't go to bed with anyone, no matter what your age. If you don't want to have a baby, that is.

If you make do with kissing and cuddling each other you can start kissing boys as soon as you like—while you're still in your pram. But far too many girls fail to realize that boys react rather differently from girls.

A boy who is sexually mature—which may well be from the age of twelve or thirteen—is not able to control himself or make do with kissing and cuddling when his sexual excitement reaches a certain point. Girls can all right. They are slower off the mark and as a rule can keep themselves under control until a much later stage in the cuddling.

A few girls start menstruating just after the age of ten, but most at about thirteen, fourteen or fifteen. Some even later.

Yes, one breast is normally a little larger than the other.

Unfortunately it's normal to be shy about talking to one's

parents. Very shy, in fact, if one hasn't been told anything or if one's parents show ignorance and a lack of understanding and are always forbidding things—but it can probably be regarded as quite natural for even the most enlightened and liberally brought-up children to get into a state of conflict with their parents during puberty or a little later. And then all confidence is destroyed too.

This can hardly be avoided in a changing society like ours, where in point of fact there are only a few years between each generation—in the sense that the new generation rejects a great many norms that were generally accepted only a few years previously.

i. & s.h.

Willing?

I'd like to know if women are just as willing to go to bed with a man as vice versa.

The answer is NO. The majority of women aren't as spontaneously keen on sex as the majority of men.

The same thing applies to animals—the males are the more impetuous, whereas the females don't start getting interested until things are under way.

But this doesn't mean there aren't women who are very keen on sex, and men who are not so keen—but they're not so common.

i. & s.h.

Older Girls

I often find myself falling in love with girls older than myself. I'm only fourteen, but look sixteen or seventeen.
Am I abnormal, or am I too shy?

We're sure you're both normal and shy, because that's normal too. But it's women aged thirty to forty who like young men. It's seldom that girls of sixteen, seventeen or eighteen fall for a fourteen-year-old.

i. & s.h.

Are Girls Like This?

I'm a young man of twenty-three, and I often feel an uncontrollable desire to have sexual intercourse with a woman. When the urge comes over me I become restless and unable to concentrate on my work. Am I the only one with this problem?

I'd also very much like to know if women have the same problem? One of my friends has been going steady with a girl for a year, and finally he more or less had to pester her to let him sleep with her.

If women exist who feel the way I do, how do I go about finding one? I mean, if you're a bit shy and not really a skirt-chaser—and not interested in getting married, because I couldn't support a wife?

Your friend should be able to tell you that he gets a bit uncontrollable now and then too. Most men have experienced this. So you are by no means the only person to have the problem.

s.h.

It's quite correct that women don't get as uncontrollable as men—generally speaking. (Of course there are men who don't get so wild, and women who get wilder than others.)

The fact that women don't get as uncontrollable has something to do with the fact that most women find it much more difficult to obtain sexual satisfaction from normal intercourse. They find it much more difficult than the majority of men.

i.h.

To a certain extent it's a question of age. Broadly speaking, women become more passionate with the years. But then again, it depends whether the woman finds a kind and imaginative and knowledgeable man who can help her here and there—especially there.

So you shouldn't run away with the idea that you can just go out and find yourself a warm-blooded, sexy girl. First and foremost you should frequent the places girls go to, clubs, dancehalls and the like—and then it's up to you to turn her into a warm-hearted, lovely girl over the years—because it takes time.

i. & s.h.

My Mother is My Rival!

I'm a nineteen-year-old girl and I live at home. I like living at home and I'm allowed to have friends in, boys and girls and so on, but—yes, there is a 'but'! My mother gets completely silly when there are young men in the house. She flirts with them quite openly, and it's embarrassing to watch, even though my boy-friends pretend to like it just to be polite. I get quite scared thinking how it may end up. After all, they're my friends.

It's not quite certain that your boy-friends are only being polite. Young men can also see some charm in motherly ladies —but of course it doesn't help your problem.

It sounds as if your mother is alone, in which case you must accept the fact that she—like all other human beings—has a need for tenderness and love. We must also accept the fact that women in their forties often have a period when they develop a fondness for young men.

But of course getting to be a proper rival is another matter. It's difficult for young people to accept parents as warm-hearted beings with lives of their own. They think that parents are 'past it' and ought to know their place, that their love-lives are ridiculous and ought to be kept tactfully concealed!

Your mother must be allowed to have a love life and somebody to be fond of. On the other hand she probably ought to hold back a bit more where your friends are concerned and assume the role of mother more. And of course she mustn't flirt with young men you yourself are interested in. That's probably the moral attitude in this society, but it doesn't make it very easy for a woman who is past the first bloom of youth.

Perhaps she's had to give up rather a lot of things on your account and now has no other opportunity of making contacts? Don't regard her as something out of the Ark, but as a woman who also has a right to live. And rejoice in the fact that your own

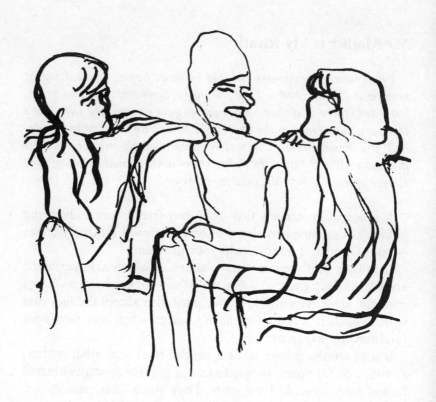

life will be full of love for the next sixty years—if you live to be eighty, for instance—providing other people give you a chance.

i. & s.h.

It Takes Two to Make a Lie

When my husband and I started going steady we talked about how lovely it was that we'd only been to bed with each other. Then we got married, and a few years later one of my husband's best friends told me some nasty stories about my husband, something to do with a girl.

I turned the problem over in my mind for quite a while and then I plucked up courage one evening and asked him if it was true. So then he said it was something he was very unhappy about and would rather forget. He was ashamed of it, and the reason he hadn't said anything to me about it when we were talking about the subject was because he was so fond of me.

The trouble is that ever since then it's been going round and round my mind. Every time we go out and I have a few drinks I start nagging at him about it and get really nasty to him.

And when we sleep together I often find myself thinking about it, and then I don't get any enjoyment out of it and don't have an orgasm and it all ends up in one big row instead.

What shall I do?

There are a couple of points we must object to. First, you write: '. . . how lovely it was we'd only been to bed with each other.' Why is it lovely? So's you can say, later on, 'If only I'd been to bed with somebody else besides my husband!'?

Then you write: 'some nasty stories about my husband.' Does the fact that he's been to bed with another girl before you have to be a 'nasty story'?

There's something very badly wrong with your outlook. It's too sentimental and romantic. It can cause repercussions of various kinds—it made your fiancé lie to you, for instance.

It takes two to make a lie: someone who can't stand up to hearing the truth, and someone who doesn't dare to speak it.

You can't build up a marriage on that sort of thing. Life and marriage are difficult enough as it is without superfluous romantics.

i. & s.h.

Filth

My problem is that I think sex in all forms is just filth, to put it bluntly. But now I've fallen in love and so I'm in a proper mess, because I daren't tell her. I can see how it's going to end up.

I've been this way ever since I was quite small. When the others wanted to play doctors and nurses I'd go off by myself, because it made me feel like being sick.

What shall I do? I'm sixteen.

It doesn't sound at all nice to feel that way. But the fact that you write to us at all indicates that you'd like to be rid of your fear of everything to do with sex.

You write: 'I can see how it's all going to end.' But is that quite true?

We assume the girl is about the same age as yourself, so it's unlikely she'll be making very severe sexual demands on you. Girls seldom do at that age. We're sure she'd be simply delighted just to sit and spoon and hold hands with you and similar innocent amusements. So that shouldn't scare you.

What is really scaring you is not her sexuality, but your own. It is you who are full of sex and interest in sex and erotic desires. Thank heavens!

But unfortunately you've been given a feeling of guilt at an early age, been made to feel afraid and ashamed of feelings and interests of this kind.

A skilful psychoanalyst would no doubt be able to help you to find the cause of the trouble, and that would reduce those silly feelings of yours which prevent you from being happy about this girl and about having fallen in love with her.

i. & s.h.

Different?

I'm a young man of twenty, and I've got a problem which perhaps isn't so very big from your viewpoint, but I'd still like to have your answer. I have a number of friends whom I've known for many years. The thing is, most of them have got engaged now, and some have got married. But I haven't found a girl yet. It's as though I just can't find anybody I can get on with. I've tried several times, but after a couple of days I break off the connection, even though the girls may be awfully sweet and pretty. I've never actually been to bed with a girl yet, and a while ago it crossed my mind I might be playing in the wrong team, and since then I haven't been able to get this thought out of my mind, even though I realize perfectly well it's just nonsense. It upsets me a good deal, for my dearest wish is to have a sweet and loving wife and a couple of nice kids. The thought crops up most frequently when I'm at work—I'm a trainee in an office—where I have time to think about things. Is it normal for a young man of my age? Ten minutes later I may well be sitting on a chair feeling grumpy for no real reason, just after having been in a good mood. It's as though I can't find my proper self. Is it normal at my age?

We can answer you very easily, but you must promise not to misunderstand our answer. We actually believe that all human beings are born more or less bi-sexual, i.e. with sexual feelings towards both their own and the opposite sex. Many things would seem to point to this. But we live in a society in which it's 'forbidden', not by law, but by an unwritten moral code, to fall in love with a person of one's own sex.

So by and large it is those who, for one reason or another, are excluded from taking an interest in the opposite sex who become pure homosexuals. And there are no more than five to ten per cent of the population of any Western country who permit themselves to become fond of persons of both sexes, i.e. are bi-sexuals.

We've written all this to help you to understand that it's not always so easy to find your natural inclination. Nature is much more versatile than us human beings when we talk about 'natural' and 'unnatural'.

It's definitely not abnormal for a young man of your age to find his mood swinging back and forth without finding a firm footing, a point of departure. We could put it this way too: it is perhaps the most talented amongst us that don't find their feet in life so very early. This doesn't make it any easier for you.

i. & s.h.

Cheated

I'm a young woman of twenty, married, with two children aged one-and-a-half and four respectively. My husband is twenty-four, and we get on well together sexually, but for the past six months or so it's as though I've had a sort of yearning for somebody else.

My husband's colleague comes here regularly, and a little while ago we were alone together for a time. We kissed, and had gone a little further, but then one of the children woke up. I've got a terrific desire to go to bed with him. It's as though it was the most important thing in life and nothing else really mattered!

For a long time I've also felt like going out and having fun by myself and having a day off away from my husband and my children and my home, just being myself.

Could it be because I got married and had my first baby when I was sixteen and so never really had a proper youth? Or is there something the matter with me?

My husband knows all about it. We've tried to find a solution, but can't. And then my husband said I was welcome to go to bed with this friend of his if it would help me to be myself again.

I just don't know what to do. It's getting on my nerves and my family is suffering because of it.

I love my husband, but I still feel this other man has something to give me. I'm quite difficult to satisfy sexually. He's twenty-five. Maybe I just need that finishing touch?

We're afraid we haven't got the ideal solution either.

It's true you've been cheated out of some of your youth, and that this is a contributory factor. But even women who have 'had their youth' feel like letting their hair down once in a while.

Going to bed with the friend is unlikely to be a good solution —not if you reckon on his continuing to come and see you in your home and stay friends with your husband! But unfortunately you're not likely to listen to us.

It would be better if you could arrange to have a day off once in a while. Or if you and your husband could have a little holiday for a day or two—separately. He could look after the children, for instance. All wives need this sort of thing.

Don't imagine that the friend will be any better at it than your husband. It is rather improbable that the first time you have sexual intercourse with a relative stranger it should prove to be better than with your husband, to whom you're accustomed.

You and your husband should read a few of the latest books on sex education and see if you and he can find a few ideas for variations. Because being married to the same person, day in and day out, is like having rissoles for every meal. What's needed is inventiveness, pickled gherkins, cranberry sauce, a sprig of parsley.

i. & s.h.

My Friend's Wife

I'm nineteen years old and often go to bed with my friend's wife. Every time she says: 'Be careful!'

I do so feel like making her pregnant. I reckon her husband would be blamed for it.

Is it true women can feel it when you make them pregnant?

You're a real pal, aren't you! We'll tell you the sort of thing that happens to pals like you.

Once upon a time, during autumn manoeuvres, two comrades-in-arms, Tom and Harry, spent the night at a farm. The farmer was dead, and his widow was very beautiful.

In the middle of the night Tom crept into the beautiful widow's bed and they had a lovely time until the early hours of the morning.

They had to leave early, and the lovely lady asked Tom what his name was, and Tom cunningly gave his comrade's name instead. 'My name's Harry,' he said. 'Oh, Harry! Harry! Harry!' whispered the beautiful widow. And she noted down Harry's name and address.

And so twenty-five years passed by, during which Tom didn't exactly prosper. He turned up in his rather shoddy clothes at his old regiment's 25th jubilee reunion, and there met his old friend Harry. 'You seem to have got on damned well!' he said to Harry enviously.

Harry removed a silver-banded meerschaum from his mouth and said: 'Yes, I have. It's a funny story. Do you remember that lovely farmer's widow we spent the night with when we were on autumn manoeuvres once? She died a few years ago and left me the farm and quite a lot of money. I wonder where the devil she got my name and address from?'

i. & s.h.

Appetite Comes With Eating

My wife, who is twenty, never feels like making love until we're actually in the middle of it. Why not?

Recently we read in your column that very few women had an orgasm during actual intercourse. Most of them only had one if the man touched or kissed their clitoris. But my wife simply can't stand having her clitoris touched with a finger. She says it's like an electric shock, and not pleasant at all.

It's a little better if I kiss her clitoris and use my tongue, but is this normal?

It's not unusual for women—especially young women—not to feel so very much sexual desire until they are 'actually in the middle of it'. We can't explain *why*, but would merely point out that the same trait is found in many animal species, namely that the female begins to take an interest only after the male has shown his interest in various ways.

There's nothing the slightest bit abnormal or unusual or wrong in your wife preferring the more sensitive, gentler touch possible with the tongue to the slightly rougher touch of the finger.

You just have to bear in mind that it all takes time. A good sexual relationship cannot be built up in the course of a week or a month. Progress is sometimes only noticeable over periods of six months or more. And, just as with all forms of development, there will be periods of stagnation and back-sliding on the way.

And sex life never becomes completely perfect. People who claim their love-making is completely perfect and devoid of problems every time must get bored to tears. But of course this is pretty thin consolation to the many who feel things are quite hopeless.

i. & s.h.

PS. But please see the next question!

Important News!

My wife can't manage to have an orgasm, either during inter-course or by means of petting. We've been married for almost five years and as far as I remember it's only happened once in all this time.

I've read everything I've been able to get hold of, but haven't found any form of instruction in the actual technique of sexual intercourse.

She says her clitoris hurts after being touched for a short time —is that normal? Incidentally she's terribly ticklish and gives a terrific jerk at the slightest touch anywhere else on her body. The effect it had on me once (when she gave one of these jerks) was that I completely lost all my desire.

She won't go and see our doctor. He can't do anything, she says. All this means we only make love together two or three times a month. This is far too little for me, and I love my wife very dearly, so I want things to be as nice as possible for her, and try not to be too selfish.

The information you give us calls for several comments.

First you don't mention whether your wife ever has an orgasm by masturbating. Your letter (which we have shortened) indicates that she may have too many inhibitions to resort to this—or to talk about it.

Your wife is otherwise (like most women of her age) backward in her sexual development, seen in relation to men. Women develop more slowly than men and only reach the height of their sexual development during their thirties, whereas men are as a rule sexually interested before they've even reached their twentieth birthday. This is a discrepancy which must be taken into account.

Books by people like Albert Ellis, for instance, can tell you quite a lot about the technique of sexual intercourse.

It sounds a little silly that you should lose your desires because your wife is very ticklish. It is possible that you are a bit too rough with her clitoris, which after all is an extremely sensitive organ (like an eyeball, but more ticklish). It needs only the very lightest of touches for a woman to notice it very strongly.

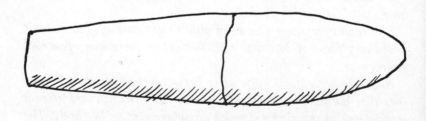

A small battery-driven vibratory massager

You must be persistent and persevering and not give up, but you must also be understanding and patient. These are big demands, we know that, but the chances of their producing results are also big.

Perhaps you should also begin to give some thought to the possibility of an electric massage machine, which has brought about a revolution in the lives of many women. It is possible that your wife will throw up her hands in horror at this proposal, but she too will get older and more liberal and frank herself, so she may be able to get used to the thought in time.

You mention that your wife complains her clitoris gets sore quickly. There *may* be a purely physical problem here, one which it is most important to be aware of. It's the sort of problem a woman must take to a doctor, possibly to a gynaecologist.

In a number of women, especially in young women, the prepuce, or foreskin on the clitoris, has more or less grown together with the clitoris itself and is thus prevented from sliding back freely. And in the little pocket which is formed a few rejected cells may collect (skin is constantly being renewed) thereby causing irritation and perhaps hurting—rather like having something in your eye—and sometimes it's impossible to clean it out properly.

It's obvious that if some foreign body has got stuck right close to the clitoris, which is extremely sensitive, the woman won't care to have anything touching her at this particular point because it will smart and be painful.

It can easily be fixed by a doctor with the help of a blunt probe, which is first inserted just above the clitoris where the *labia minora* meet, and then sort of flicked down along one side of the clitoris—and then down along the other side. Downwards and *outwards*. In this way the adhesion can be overcome.

(It will be necessary to take this detailed description along to the gynaecologist in order to show exactly what is meant.)

It's not very pleasant, but it doesn't really hurt that much. If necessary the doctor can use a small amount of local anaesthetic.

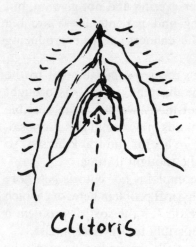

Both these schematic drawings show the part just above the woman's vagina. In the middle is a normal clitoris from which the prepuce, or foreskin, can glide back freely. On either side are the smaller vaginal lips, and outside them the larger ones.

Clitoris

This drawing shows how the prepuce may have difficulty in gliding back. The doctor then has to use the right-hand end of the probe, also shown here, and inserts it just above the clitoris where the smaller vaginal lips meet, and more or less flicks it outwards and downwards to loosen the prepuce—on either side of the clitoris.

Clitoris

When the doctor has performed this very small operation, it's important to make sure adhesion doesn't occur again. So every morning and evening for a while afterwards—say a week or two —the woman should draw back (downwards) the foreskin on the clitoris so that the clitoris itself is exposed, and then smear a little cold cream (or Vaseline or the like) on the actual shaft of the clitoris until the two surfaces, which have been dragged apart from each other and are a little rough, have healed and become smooth so that they won't stick together again.

It is only when this little operation has been performed that the woman will stand a chance of washing herself properly in all these little crevices—and the hypersensitivity and irritability will disappear.

It is not so very long ago that it was discovered that an adhesion of this kind could produce problems in connection with titillation of the clitoris, so there will be a number of doctors who haven't heard about it yet.

But it should be stressed that it is not a problem for all women. It *can*, however, be the reason if a woman, despite very gentle touching of the clitoris, still complains of soreness.

And this little operation, as we've mentioned, is not so very troublesome, so it may well be worth a try to see if this is the cause of the irritation.

Finally it should be added that this problem should remind all women how important it is to keep the clitoris and the area surrounding it completely clean, that whatever is employed to tickle the clitoris is clean—and not too dry.

i. & s.h.

A Kind of Virgin

I'm a girl of sixteen, and I've got problems which may not sound much to others, but I go through a struggle with myself every day as to what I should do.

I've got lots of friends and go to a lot of parties. I'm sure you know how these parties usually end up. Among my friends it's

quite common to go to bed with each other—I don't mean every-
body with everybody—and this is where the trouble lies.

About six months ago I had sexual intercourse for the first time,
but I don't think all my maidenhead was removed, so I'm still a
kind of virgin. I've tried again a couple of times since, but it hurts
so much every time I have to stop.

Why? Before my menstruation I never have any more than
ordinary tummy-aches. Is it because I'm not patient enough that
the membrane hasn't broken?

Apart from which I don't feel like going to bed with anybody,
and I don't get any pleasure out of it either. I suppose I'm not old
enough? I also got scared by the first time, because I'd thought it
was going to be lovely, and it wasn't lovely at all.

I don't mind petting (what does it actually mean?), even like it,
but when a boy wants to go any further I have to tell him to pack
it in. Does it matter to a boy?

Does a boy get any fun out of putting his fingers up a girl's
vagina? Does a boy get any fun out of having a girl kiss his penis?
And is it peculiar if I think it's revolting?

There are thousands of other things I'd like to ask you about,
but it would take too much of your time. But it's been really lovely
to get some of these things off my chest.

I can't talk to my mother about them, and that's why I've
written to you as though you were my mother.

It sounds so easy to answer you by saying: 'When you don't
feel like going to bed with a boy, don't!'

But it would be a pointless answer, because you naturally
experience a certain pressure from the other members of your
group—and from boys you may be fond of. But there's no harm
in sticking to petting—for one thing there's no risk of ending
up with a baby.

Petting means fondling and caressing each other in every
possible way except having proper intercourse, i.e. without the
man's penis coming anywhere near the woman's vagina. In this
way no sperm gets up into the vagina and you don't get pregnant.

If you feel pain when having intercourse it's probably because you're anxious and afraid of this new and exciting and dangerous and unknown thing that seems to be on everybody's mind the whole time.

Like so many other girls, you have heard about this wonderful thing called sexual intercourse. And you think, like the rest of us have thought too at one time, that as long as you lean back and spread your legs wide this wonderful experience will come marching along all by itself. Boys and men have such an easy time of it, but girls and women have to work so much harder to reach the wonderful climax known as orgasm.

You should also learn that women's sexual maturity comes slowly, whereas boys are at the height of their virility between the ages of fifteen and twenty. This means that a woman's interest in sex gets stronger and stronger from the age of twelve or thirteen (sometimes earlier) until she is thirty or forty. It is only when she is about thirty-five or so that a woman is fully developed sexually and likely to be most interested in sex. This is just the general picture—not all women are precisely the same.

As a rule, men are most keenly interested in having sexual intercourse between the ages of fifteen and twenty, so in a way one might say that, sexually speaking, very young men are most suited to youngish women of thirty to forty—and in fact it is by no means rare for young men to learn a great deal from a relationship with a more mature woman.

So you're not the slightest bit abnormal. Most women would agree with everything you describe. The pain during sexual intercourse comes, as already mentioned, because you are afraid and tense your muscles.

There is something else you should know that is very important—something very few young women realize: a woman can kiss and cuddle sexually with a man and can literally stop whenever she likes—without any difficulty. But when a man has got even a little bit sexually excited it's very difficult for him to back out of things and stop. He very quickly and very easily becomes so wild the girl can hardly recognize him.

A boy or a man likes a girl to fondle his penis in various ways

—it's one of the many forms of petting—and can easily be made to ejaculate in this way. And then the wildness stops.

Most boys and men are keenest on getting their penis into the girl's vagina, but the other method also has many advantages. Petting is also, in point of fact, an excellent form of 'preliminary training' prior to sexual relations proper later on. In this way the two persons can get to know each other without any great risk—as long as they are careful not to let any sperm from the man's penis get near the girl's vagina.

You must realize that it takes time for two people to get accustomed to each other sexually, because most women have a harder time getting to the point of orgasm than most men.

I hope this letter will have answered most of your questions. I think most women will understand when they read this letter —including your own mother.

i.h.

I'm Only Asking

Could you help me with some problems which I don't feel like discussing with anybody else? I'll be eighteen in a month's time and haven't got any particular boy-friend. My first problem is that now and then, especially during the last two weeks before my menstruation, I feel a burning desire to have sexual intercourse. This longing has only come during the last year or so, but has been getting more and more intense. It started when, for the first time, I experienced sexual relations as something beautiful and irre-placeable—I just hadn't realized such a thing existed and was taken completely by surprise. This was with a twenty-one-year-old young man whom I've unfortunately seen on this one occasion only.

And this is where my second problem arises. It's against all the principles and moral codes to sleep with a person you've only known for a single evening or at least normally don't associate with. But why? Isn't it acceptable for a girl to have a sexual craving in the same way as a man, and for sexual relations to be beautiful and rewarding even if you don't love each other? Why do people insist on there being a connection between love and sexual pleasure? Why do many boys look down on a girl who 'says OK' the very first evening? Why do her girl-friends get shocked and start talking about 'tartiness' when the person who has experienced it happens to find it beautiful and rewarding?

Why is it something for a man to be proud of and a girl to be ashamed of?

Perhaps you will feel the whole problem is trivial if I tell you that by sexual relations I don't necessarily mean sexual intercourse proper. But from a moral viewpoint, surely the problem is more or less the same? Does a girl really have to go round feeling guilty and ashamed of herself, and is she really less worthy because, even though she doesn't happen to have any kind of 'steady' partner, she nevertheless experiences a sexual urge and tries to satisfy it?

My third problem is that, despite a great desire, I don't dare start a regular sexual relationship with anybody, partly because I'm afraid of getting pregnant (I've still got many years of study ahead of me), and partly because most people think it's very wrong to have sexual relations with somebody who is not your regular boy-friend. So I'm beginning to wonder if it's me that's immoral and irresponsible.

Can I get a dutch cap, or, better, the really safe pills, without my parents' knowledge? In which case do I have to go and be measured by my regular doctor? If not now, can I get it as soon as I'm eighteen?

We think your letter and your questions are extremely wise and sensible.

The craving for sexual relations (and you're quite right, it doesn't have to be sexual intercourse proper) *can* make itself felt during specific periods, as in your case.

You are quite right in saying that the official moral code favours men at the expense of women. You must help to change this situation. On the other hand we can't advise you to disregard the sillier aspects of this moral code completely either—and you don't.

You are also right in saying that there is absolutely no need for any connection to exist between love and sexual satisfaction. This has been acknowledged in practice as far as men are concerned, but not in respect of women, and this is unreasonable.

There are various advisory centres where you can be measured for a pessary, or dutch cap, besides going to your own doctor. You can also ask at these places about oral contraceptives, i.e. the Pill, and IUDs (intrauterine devices) such as the Margulies spiral. But all sorts of developments are taking place nowadays concerning this whole question.

i. & s.h.

Does One Have to be in Love?

A number of us have been discussing whether you can go to bed with each other without being in love.
What do you think?

We think you can, but we'd better go into the question a bit more deeply.

We gather that the question is being posed by a group of young people, and that it therefore might also be formulated in this way: 'Can a girl permit herself to go to bed with a young man without being in love with him?' It's not so much of a problem for young men.

We believe there's no reason why girls shouldn't. We know that lots of young men think it's quite all right for men to get themselves lots of experience, but that girls should stay pure while waiting for 'the one and only man in their lives'.

It's a false, dishonest and hypocritical attitude. The most intelligent of the men also say: 'We know! But that's how we happen to feel.'

(In other words, girls must face the fact that they will expose themselves to criticism if they say, as we do: 'There's no reason why we shouldn't go to bed with a man without being in love with him.')

We believe that the other attitude, i.e. that a girl simply must be in love in order to do so, involves a number of dangerous aspects. Sometimes girls go to bed with a man just because they let their emotions get the better of them. In such cases it's unfortunate if they feel they simply must persuade themselves that these feelings are love. It creates unnecessary difficulties for both parties.

Both men and women, from quite an early age, feel a need for sexual relations in the same way as they feel a need for food and drink—and it is a need which craves satisfaction, or at least an attempt to satisfy it.

(Many people as a rule feel shocked or insulted by the fact that we like to juxtapose sexual needs with other material needs, but then that's the way things are. However, apart from sexual needs, there is, of course, also the need for tenderness, romance, infatuation and various other things.)

But there is another, completely different situation, one which those who have posed this question have perhaps not thought about, namely that of the married woman. There's no problem for a married man. He can easily feel attracted by his wife— without feeling himself to be directly in love with her. (We must just mention that even in the best and happiest of marriages you can't go round being in love with each other morning, noon and night. In the best marriages you're in love with each other at intervals of varying length.)

Well, then. We know it's a problem for many married women, the fact that they don't always feel like going to bed with their husbands—because they don't happen to be in love with him at the particular moment he chooses to make gay advances with a gleam in his eye.

It is important for all these women to realize that there is no reason why they should not, in a relatively cold and cynical way, make use of their husbands as an aid to securing their own sexual satisfaction. And thus without thinking they have to work up a feeling of being in love which circumstances don't permit.

All this naturally presupposes that the man and woman in question have worked out a form of sexual togetherness that gives both of them satisfaction.

That wasn't perhaps quite what you were asking about, but it is relevant to the answer.

i. & s.h.

Can You ...

Can you make a woman or a girl feel like going to bed with you just by kissing her?

It depends *how* you kiss, and *where*.

i. & s.h.

11. Consumer Guide

Information Please!

What about a spot of plain speaking?

Seeing that the manufacturers of massage machines or vibrators and other appliances don't dare—or aren't allowed to—why don't you let us have a spot of forthright consumer guidance? Incidentally, now that at long last they've manufactured something which, compared with vacuum-cleaners and other appliances, must be termed an even more useful apparatus, isn't it rather unfortunate that the design seems to be based on the superstitious myth about vaginal orgasms?

Thanks for your letter. We shall try to give some idea of the range of vibrators and other appliances on the market.*

We've worked our way through mountains of massage machines of different kinds and can report as follows. There are non-electric types (massage rollers, for example) and electric ones. We believe that only the electric ones will be of any interest in the present connection. Single men and women can also derive great pleasure from the majority of these electric vibrators.

Electric massage machines, vibratory massagers or vibrators —as they are variously called—are harmless, effective and no more habit-forming than a few other nice things such as

---

* We'd like to draw attention to the fact that a person who happens to be a mail order customer of a shop for special appliances runs the risk of having his or her name and address sold to other dealers. In the United States, for example, fifty addresses of this kind may be sold for $10 or more. Of course this may well be an advantage, but then there are people who place only one order, after which they don't necessarily wish to be contacted again. And some like to decide for themselves whom they are going to receive catalogues from. It is probably advisable, when placing orders with these shops, to state quite clearly whether one wants to have one's name and address sold to somebody else or not—and then sit back and hope one's wishes will be complied with!

chocolate and visits to fun fairs. They are available in electrical shops, 'surgical appliance' shops and some chemists.

We haven't seen any that seem capable of giving dangerous electric shocks. And of course the battery-driven ones don't stand a chance of doing so.

But even the massage machines and vibrators provided with a lead and a plug for an electric point don't seem to present any sort of danger—unless of course they're actually dipped in water. But they would appear to be able to tolerate ordinary dampness without being dangerous. Not that it would be a good idea to take them into the bath with you. If you're in your bath a shower nozzle is much better.

1. *Massage machines for plugging into an electric point.* As a rule these are more expensive than the battery-driven vibrators, and heavier, and have a selection of attachments that are of little importance in this connection—for massaging your scalp, your face and all that sort of thing. These machines often have two or more speeds, which means you can try out a weaker as

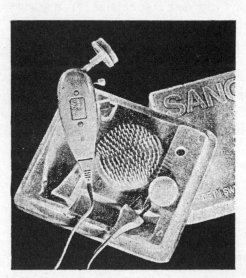

A cheap, light vibratory massager with a switch for gradually adjusting speed.

well as a more powerful kind of stimulation. The majority of massage machines in this group (with a lead and plug) will probably be suitable for most people.

2. *Battery-driven massage machines* (*vibrators, stimulators*). Very small ones are obtainable, about 4 in. long, in plastic. They are handy, effective and by far the cheapest. Perhaps a little smooth to hold. A wash-leather sheath, for instance, would probably make them easier to handle. There are several different models. Those we have seen have all been of Japanese origin. The large vibrators are slightly more than normal penis-size and shape—even if one imagines a penis in full flower. They are about 6 or 7 in. long and 1½ to 1¾ in. in diameter. We agree with our letter-writer's remark that they seem to be designed to be inserted into the vagina.

The vagina is relatively insensitive to things that jab or cut—no pain spots—but vibration and deeper pressure are sensations which the vagina is perfectly capable of registering.

But no matter what kind of massage machine is used, the right place to massage is still the clitoris, the little button just above the entrance to the vagina.

As a rule it's so effective that most men get jealous and insist on being allowed to hold the machine and direct it themselves. But very few men indeed—presumably no man at all—is as skilful as the woman in question when it comes to controlling the progress of the massage. So we would advise men to control themselves instead (so to speak) and enjoy themselves for instance with their penis inside the woman's vagina at the same time, in which case there may be a chance of achieving what is otherwise so very difficult and rare, namely: *simultaneous orgasm*, i.e. when the man ejaculates and the woman has an orgasm at the same time.

In the case of the man, it is especially the head of the penis, known as the *glans*, that can be stimulated by massage with an electric vibrator. In many cases it can cure a lack of stiffness, i.e. an unsatisfactory erection.

No wonder that these useful little contrivances have been a tremendous success in Japan (where many of them are also made), in the United States and many other places all over the world.

Most of the foregoing applies to all types of massage machine. But to get back to the stick-shaped (penis-shaped or 'personal' vibrators as they are generally known): as a rule they come in two designs, namely one-speed models and two-speed models.

Of course it's a slight advantage not to have to worry about having a power plug—in fact in some cases it's a great advantage.

The big vibrators are also made of smooth, relatively hard plastic (so are the kinds you plug into the main electric supply) and as a rule are grooved and thus easy to handle.

Many people may smile at all this, but the fact remains that these vibrators can mean a revolution in the sex lives of many single people as well as married couples. Which means they are very important. (Both Masters and Johnson and other American doctors say they have used massage machines for treating sexual difficulties, and that they recommend them for more routine use in the home too.)

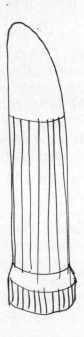

A 'personal vibratory massager'.
Made of hard plastic, battery driven.

A very well-known, clever, experienced and respected doctor has told us that once in a while he has women patients who, after many years of marriage, come to see him and tell him they are frigid. Now there is no such thing as a frigid woman, but that's what they believe.

He makes them lie down on the couch and places a buzzing massage machine on their clitoris. They start wriggling and jerking about delightedly, most surprised, and admit they feel all sorts of things. 'Which only shows you're not frigid,' he notes drily. 'Please note that I haven't kissed you, murmured sweet words, caressed you or made advances of any kind. I've merely placed this impersonal, professional piece of equipment on the right spot—and you immediately feel more than you ever thought you'd be capable of feeling. *Voilà!*'

The fact that some of these massage machines are so clearly penis-shaped is due, as our correspondent points out, to the misunderstanding about vaginal orgasms (which don't exist). But then the idea is probably more to indicate, in a smart and elegant fashion, their sexual usefulness. This is probably why they are the ones which sell best—though the price of course plays a part too.

i. & s.h.

Reward!

You've written so often about massage machines, which can be such a splendid help to women during intercourse, but there must be other things.

I've been collecting various things for many years, and I've got french letters with portraits of famous persons on them, and others with coxcombs and fancy protuberances of one kind and another. I've got penis extensions made of rubber and gadgets that can be drawn on to the penis with the object of stimulating the clitoris a little more effectively.

So I'm always on the look out for gadgets and gimmicks of all types that people with imagination and a sense of humour have dreamt up in the course of time—private inventions as well as mass-produced aids.

All sorts of brilliant inventions must have been made—and deserve wider publicity. So please, Mr and Mrs Hegeler, couldn't you ask your readers to tell you about any ideas, aids, gadgets, etc. that can help to make sexual relations more fun?

By all means!

We're all for appealing to our readers on this subject. In fact we're prepared to offer a reward to the best contribution(s).

We can start by mentioning a couple of examples.

1. This bears the romantic name 'Happy End', and is a kind of folded rubber brush of the type used for suede leather, provided with a ring so that it can be worn down at the root of the penis. The idea, quite simply, is that the soft little rubber

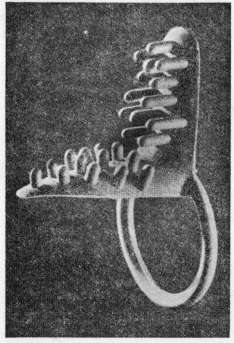

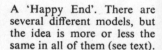

A 'Happy End'. There are several different models, but the idea is more or less the same in all of them (see text).

'bristles' can stimulate the woman's clitoris during ordinary intercourse with the penis inside the vagina.

How effective it is is hard to say. Some people will find it very effective. It greatly increases the stimulation of the woman's most sensitive parts. This and the other gadgets mentioned in this chapter—apart from vibrators—are more easily obtained by mail order direct from suppliers than from shops.

2. A 'penis-enlarger'. As is well known, the majority of men are dissatisfied with their own penis and feel it is too small. We have often mentioned that this is an entirely unreasonable and unfounded attitude, and that the penis is not nearly so important to the woman as men think. And that a man with a small penis may well be a much more skilful and more welcome lover than a man with a large penis. But superstitions are very hard to eradicate, and no doubt we'll be bombarded, unfortunately, with questions about where this gadget can be purchased, although the 'Happy End' is probably much better.

The penis is inserted into the apparatus and held firmly in position by pressing the rubber bulb a few times. Models can even be supplied with rubber testicles—which in turn can be filled with water so that the penis can squirt when its user feels in a gay mood.

On the left is a thick french letter made of rubber and provided with a kind of coxcomb that increases stimulation of the clitoris. It's even called a *Clitorex*. The one on the right has a hard lump on the end which serves to extend the penis (we're dubious about its effect). Both are sold at very high prices.

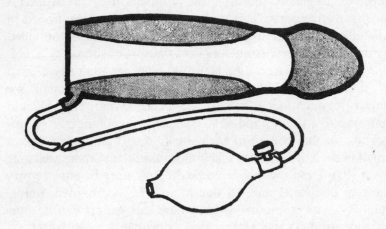

A German inflatable partial dummy penis with valve. It is also possible to buy french letters in various thicknesses and with various forms of extension. But, we repeat, greeting your girl-friend with a king-size penis (whether genuine or made of rubber) isn't necessarily going to ensure perfect bliss.

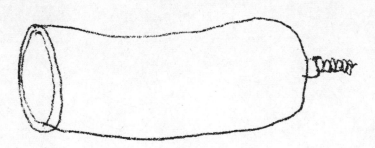

An artificial vagina for the delight of lonely men. Self-operative, in the sense that at the right-hand end it can be connected up to a massage machine (the kind provided with a lead for plugging into the mains and various fittings which can be screwed on as desired). The price is exorbitant.

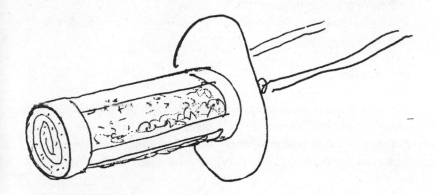

This apparatus is called a 'surgical support' and is designed to be strapped on. The idea is that a very small penis can be rolled up in foam rubber and placed inside the stiffening framework. The price of this apparatus is more reasonable.

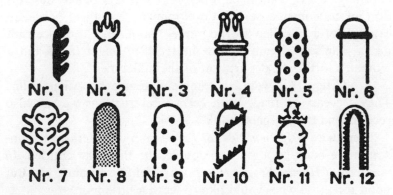

The value of these fanciful German condoms to the ladies is slight. On the other hand their psychological value is undeniable. Many men find them enchanting, and some of them are obtainable in various colours. However, they have been known to give a woman cramp—not in her vaginal, but her facial muscles.

We'd like to stress that all ideas are welcome. It cannot be denied that even gadgets whose practical effect is limited may well have a psychological effect.

i. & s.h.

Sex Books

You often recommend people to go and get books on sex education at the library and study them. And very right of you too. But then you also advise against all the ignorance and superstition displayed by both the ostensibly 'educational' and other books on sex.

We realize you can't very well recommend your own books and your own excellent gramophone record (which can sometimes be hard to get hold of), but couldn't you name a couple of books, not only of the directly instructional type, but also amongst the so-called 'pornographic' ones, that meet with your approval?

Well, there's a rather suggestive-looking book that's better than its title and cover, namely *Am I An Erotomaniac?* by Rey Anthony. We've mentioned it before. It's a very honest description of a woman's sexual development, in other words an example of a so-called 'pornographic' book, that for once isn't just a man's daydream of how he feels 'it' ought to be, but a woman's forthright description of the difficulties.

In addition, we would recommend books by Albert Ellis. They are easy to read. With certain reservations we can also recommend the Rainers' book.

Then there is *Human Sexual Response* by Masters and Johnson and a book by a married couple, the Brechers, entitled *An Analysis of Human Sexual Reactions*. Scientific reading, yes. But good for those who would like to learn a little more.

Julius Fast has written a book called *Sexual Enjoyment*, also dealing with the inquiry into the sexual habits of human beings conducted by Masters and Johnson.

i. & s.h.

PS. For many years Kinsey's reports were the bible of sexual enlightenment. Now, justifiably, the bible is Masters and Johnson's work, published in 1966.

NB. As far as pornographic books are concerned, we make a distinction between two categories:

1. Those which try to create sexual excitement. As a rule they are utterly dishonest, merely men's daydreams about how things might be. But they are better, cheaper and more fun than going to see a doctor and having expensive hormone injections. In other words, useful in their way. The trouble about them is that they provide an entirely false impression of other people's sex lives.

2. Honest (literary) descriptions of human beings and their sexual relationships. They are seldom as exciting as the first category. On the other hand they are more instructive. There aren't many of them on the market as yet, but when bans on pornography are lifted it is only to be hoped that excellent things will emerge in due course.

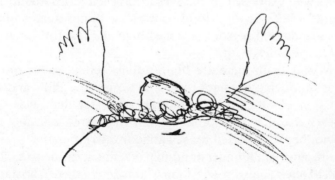

This is the sort of view a grown man has of himself and his penis if he looks downwards and his stomach isn't in the way. It doesn't impress him, and when he glances at other men he can't help forming the misleading impression that his own is a small, insignificant little thing. The problem is one which concerns most men—even those who know quite well that size is quite unimportant.

For or Against the Pill?

I have an excellent and generally liberal-minded woman doctor in whom I have placed my faith for the past twenty years.

Now I feel I'd like to go over to the Pill, but you'd think I'd given her an electric shock when I mentioned it to her. She advised me against it very strongly, among other reasons because of the risk of a blood-clot on the brain, particularly in the case of a middle-aged woman (I'm forty-two).

So now I just don't know what to do. Of course she can't refuse to give me a prescription for the Pill. On the other hand she's not likely to be very cooperative if problems should arise.

I actually thought the risk was greatest for younger women who might want to have children later. What do you think?

We think your doctor is taking an unduly black view of things.

When oral contraceptives—or 'the Pill'—first appeared and were tested, there were a number of over-moral scientists and doctors who expressed themselves in shocked terms about these 'joy pills'—because they do of course ease things tremendously. These scandalized persons searched high and low for something to scare the ladies with.

Now and again there are big headlines telling us we run the risk of producing hermaphrodites if we use the Pill—and that the risk of blood-clots on the brain is greater than ever—and whatever else they can think up. But these are *assertions*, and have not been supported by scientific investigations.

We're sure you'll understand that it's much easier to exclaim 'Don't! They're dangerous!' than 'Calm down, there's no danger in oral contraceptives!'

To be able to say that a thing is harmless it is actually necessary to know thousands of people who have used the thing in question for generations. Oral contraceptives have not been tested this long—but millions of women of twenty, thirty, forty and up towards the fifties have been using the Pill for many years now and are still using it. If it were known with any certainty that there was any risk attached, its use would have been prohibited long ago.

(We're speaking here about *healthy* women. There are certain diseases which can make it inadvisable to take oral contraceptives, but a doctor should know all about these.)

So now then. Show your doctor this question and our answer and then ask her if you come into any of the categories of sick women who shouldn't take the Pill. The point about your age is nonsense and we can only presume it's something you've misunderstood—otherwise your doctor has been badly informed.

Recently we received a private letter from a woman who, like you, had gone to see her doctor for a prescription for the Pill. The doctor had scared her out of her wits by saying: 'I wouldn't dream of it! Do you really want to become frigid? Would you like to find yourself waddling around all fat and get cancer?'

This is a very irresponsible remark for a doctor to make.

As we say, the Pill is used by millions of women all over the world, and certain particularly watchful people will be quick enough to pipe up if any risk should be detected. This should be the best guarantee we have.

So far the only truth that has been found amongst all the frightening claims is that most women put on a few pounds and bulge a little here and there or find their flesh gets a bit firmer. But they don't get cancer or blood-clots or go frigid. On the contrary.

Psychologically, there is one thing about the Pill that should be appreciated: as we mentioned earlier, it's a 'joy pill'—and what's more, a pill that can intensify sexual pleasure. And of course this is sinful and punishable—according to our old, firmly lodged sex taboo, to which we all more or less conform. The result is that women who start taking the Pill very easily become a little uneasy.

If they find they've got a sore throat they think: 'Heavens, it's probably my punishment for taking the Pill!' Or a pimple on one shoulder: 'Oh, it's probably because I'm taking the Pill!' In other words, a bit of a bad conscience about being able to enjoy sexual relations more serenely.

It's the same sex taboo that causes some doctors to react more strongly than they're supposed to. It's understandable, and it's human—but it's not *medically* correct.

The Pill really is a relief to many women. It's a shame if taboos and superstitions have to frighten anybody away from accepting the opportunity.

i. & s.h.

In a Way

I've got an overwhelming problem. It's quite impossible for me to have an orgasm with my husband. We've been married for seven years, and I've never experienced this sensation which is said to be so lovely.

We've tried a lot of things, including being very open-minded, i.e. having sexual relations with another married couple. But it still hasn't helped. I've been to doctors and psychiatrists and been given pills and injections, but nothing did me any good.

We were just about to give up the whole business when I read an answer of yours in your column to a woman who had precisely the same problem as myself. You mentioned that many women obtained great pleasure from an electric vibrator, and I took one home with me on approval. And just imagine—it worked!

But now I've got another problem, because I feel it's so dreadfully unnatural, and my husband feels the same way. I hardly dare to use it because I'm so afraid of becoming dependent upon it—or is it only a temporary solution?

To think you'd just worked out a happy ending to your story, and then you immediately have to go and find yourself a new problem! What a shame!

You mustn't feel you're doing something unnatural, and you needn't be afraid of becoming dependent upon it.

It's easy enough for us to say this, but we've had quite a number of letters like yours. Others have also mentioned that their husbands become jealous of the machine's efficacy. Others say that they are best able to direct the stimulation, and that this offends their husbands. And several are afraid of becoming dependent, just like yourself, and feel it's dreadfully artificial.

We can only repeat, again and again, that you mustn't be afraid, and that it's your right. You have the right to explore yourself, and it's an excellent aid for a time, but it may well be quite a long time, and then you'll discover something else, and then you'll revert to a third thing, and then the first, and then to something new again. Don't cling to 'normal intercourse' as a goal. It's just as silly as claiming that the only proper way to eat is with chopsticks.

i. & s.h.

Different Positions . . .?

I'm a man of thirty-nine, and my wife is thirty-seven. We've been married for fifteen years and have three lovely children. Our problem from the outset has been that my wife hasn't got anything out of the sexual side of things.

There's one aspect you haven't written about much, and which is still a problem for us, and that is the different positions for love-making.

At one time and another you've said that the man should use his tongue to titillate the woman's clitoris, and we've got a lot of pleasure out of this—my wife in particular, of course. But then her pleasure has been mine too, so to speak.

You have written about vibrators, and said that they can be a good and effective means of stimulating a woman sexually—and this has been a success too. But what is the best way to use the thing? How do you lie, who works it, and how does the man come into the picture, if I might put it that way? And have you got a suggestion for a good '69' combination?

We're only too happy to comply with your request and will therefore now, in as much detail as possible, complete with illustrations, describe a few effective positions for you. You're quite right, it is a sphere we have neglected a little.

We can't promise you 'twenty different positions' (in case you remember the old song), but just three good ones that are not so well known. They may sound a little complicated, but then we've described them very fully. Take the book along to bed with you the first couple of times and get yourselves entwined according to the instructions. You'll soon get the hang of it.

It's much easier than judo, ju-jitsu and karate—and more human, too.

Back-and-side position with vibrator

As far as we can see, this is the most effective position. *The elementary position* is what we might call it, though it's most

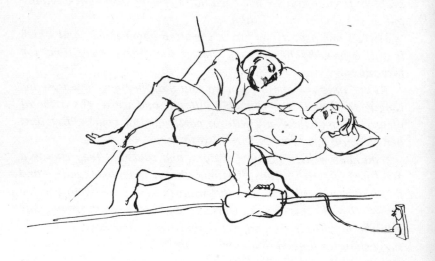

Back-and-side position with massager. The couple are seen from the foot-end of their bed. The woman is lying across the bed and the man is almost at right angles to her. (See text.)

Back-and-side position with massager. The couple are now seen from a standing position at the side of the bed. The man can have his left arm as shown here, but he can also lie slightly less on his side with his arm to the front. (See text).

certainly for advanced students too. The woman lies comfortably on her back in a big bed or comfortably and softly on the floor with plenty of cushions and eiderdowns and anything else she likes to make her comfy.

She spreads her legs apart and bends her knees.

The man lies on her right on his left side with a couple of pillows or cushions under his head. (On her right if he's right-handed, on her left if he's left-handed.)

They don't lie beside each other: there's quite a pronounced angle between them. In other words their heads are quite far apart, but the lower part of the man's body and his penis are close in to the woman's vagina.

His left leg rests, slightly bent, under her left leg, which is also bent.

His right leg passes under her right leg. Her right leg rests on his thigh, and he rests his right foot on something or other that is higher than the surface they are lying on. It may be the wall, if they are lying on the floor, or the foot-end of the bed if they're lying across the bed. If necessary he can put a cushion under his foot in case it should start going to sleep.

Now both partners are lying ready, comfortable and relaxed. His right hand is free and can take part in various things, and she has both hands free.

Neither of them should be resting their weight on the other except that the woman has the inside of her right thigh against the upper side of his right thigh, or hip. But this shouldn't overburden anybody.

The woman can now, peacefully and quite relaxed, use an electric vibrator (obtainable battery-driven or for plugging into a switch) with one hand, while with the fingers of the other she

Back-and-side position with massager. Here we are sitting at the head of the couple's bed. (See text.)

can spread the smaller vaginal lips apart. Or she can use her usual masturbation technique.

The man can get at the woman's vagina without being in the way. His right hand is free to guide his penis with, to caress the woman—or to do whatever he likes. Or whatever she likes.

This is probably one of the best positions, one that offers the most possibilities, makes the fewest demands and provides the greatest chance of satisfaction.

It may not, in itself, be so very exciting for the man, but it has advantages from his point of view too. The position can be maintained for a very long time, and if he should ejaculate before the woman has finished he still has a chance of continuing the stimulation with his fingers and hand, in other words stimulation of the entrance to the woman's vagina and the foremost third of the vagina, by means of which the clitoris can be stimulated from below as well.

In this position the man can also stimulate the woman's backside and the area round her anus, which is richly provided with nerves. Our artist's drawings show this position from three different angles.

It must be added that, of course, this position is not the most ideal for all couples—tastes vary, after all, from one person to the next. But it is probably the position which most people could agree to call satisfying.

Stimulation of the woman only, with the tongue (cunnilingus)

It is generally agreed that this is the most satisfying position for the woman. She should lie on a solid, steady table that has been made soft and comfortable with a quilt or the like. The lower part of her body should be right out by the edge of the table, her feet resting pleasantly on the arms of a comfortable chair in which the man sits. He can now pass his arms under her bent knees and rest them freely on the table. In this position the man is able to use both hands, to caress the woman, for instance. Here again, he can stimulate the woman's vagina and other orifices according to her instructions.

But the important thing is for the man to be at a good angle so that he can stimulate the woman's clitoris with his tongue.

Once again it's important to stress this point—according to the woman's instructions. She's the one who's supposed to be stimulated, and hers are the wishes that count. A demand is thus also made on the woman: she must tell the man how she wants it done—and on the man to comply with her instructions without foolish vanity.

There may be problems—finding the right height of table, the right chair—but here false modesty shouldn't prevent him or her from arranging things comfortably for themselves and experimenting and taking the trouble to see that everything is pleasant and comfortable and practical.

In this position, then, both partners concentrate on the woman's satisfaction. When she has reached her climax, it will, as a rule, have a wonderfully exciting effect on the man, who can then insert his penis into her vagina and finish off.

In cases where both partners are very advanced and skilful, the woman may be capable of having several orgasms—one or two more—perhaps even more. But as we say, it calls for years of training and adjustment.

'69', lying on the side

Many women can find it difficult to concentrate on more than one thing at a time. But this position doesn't make any special demands on either partner.

Both lie on their sides, their heads facing in opposite directions. Both rest their heads on the other person's right thigh (assuming they are both lying on their right sides). The man has his right arm over the woman's right leg, but can still use this arm a little. His left arm is free.

The man can stimulate the woman's clitoris with his tongue, and she can stimulate his penis with her mouth and tongue (*fellatio*) while at the same time caressing his body, his scrotum, his behind and others things with her hands.

It's not a position to be recommended if a woman has difficulty in reaching her climax. In this case, the first two positions described above are better. But it's an excellent position for preliminary love-play—as is the second position just described—because of the three it's the one which offers the man the greatest rewards.

Once more it must be mentioned that tastes differ, but that these remarks apply to a large number of people.

Incidentally, all three positions are excellent for pregnant women during the last three months of their pregnancy, also for the no-longer-so-young who like to lie comfortably without having to expend too much energy. Corpulent people will also find these positions rewarding.

i. & s.h.

The Clothes Line . . .

I live in a very small provincial town where everybody gossips about everybody else, and if you haven't got anything to gossip about you invent something.

'69'—cunnilingus and fellatio in combination. Both partners rest on each other's thighs. (See text.)

I would like to spare my neighbours and my neighbours'
neighbours the trouble of going to the latter extreme. I've read
somewhere or other that you can buy panties with the days of the
week embroidered on them. They're said to be terrifically chic—
especially on a clothes line in a very small provincial town . . .

Where can I buy them? And—if you happen to know—what
does a set of this kind cost?

Of course you must have panties with the days of the week on
them! They can be bought in many places. There's a very wide
selection of imaginatively designed panties on the market
nowadays.

I wonder if you ever heard that cabaret song to the effect that
people are perhaps more exciting below the surface than one
might think at first? Isn't it encouraging to think that the
Smiths and the Jacksons and the Dinglebothams are actually
quite ingenious beneath that dull mask we all see? Other people's
sex lives are fortunately not so empty and unimaginative as one
might think when we see them and hear them talk.

This is nice to know, but we shouldn't exaggerate our delight.
Because are they imaginative *enough*?

It's probably fair enough to claim that all those who marry
say to themselves, 'This is going to last!' Don't we all marry in
the firm conviction that this business of being married is something we're going to make a go of—together?

Even so, it's hard to be married.

If we marry at the age of twenty-five and live to be seventy-five,
it means we've got fifty years of sex life together. It's our duty to
take a little trouble over it! It's not quite enough just to be the
same girl and the same man to each other throughout a long
life.

Sometimes, in the course of life, we catch sight of a man or a
woman we think looks more exciting than the man or woman
we have been allotted. It's an unequal struggle, and the one who
is left behind often thinks: 'What could I have done? Why
wasn't I exciting enough?'

All too many men and women assume that everything in the

garden is lovely . . . but in a marriage it's not enough just to lie peacefully beside one another.

All too many women kill their husbands' imaginativeness and playful suggestions with raised eyebrows and a mental rap on the knuckles.

i. & s.h.

12. 'There are other things in the world besides sex'

It's a sentence we often hear. Of course there are other things in the world besides sex—even though we can't always call to mind exactly *what*.

But here, at any rate, are a few questions that are not directly concerned with sexual problems. About rules for marriage, bad-tempered customers, problems at work—and other things.

Help—She's Leaving Me!

You must help me quickly. I've known a wonderful girl for a couple of years. As a matter of fact we've been living together as man and wife.

And then, just before Christmas, she tells me she's going to leave me, that she's fallen in love with somebody else. Admittedly there's a glimmer of hope—she's gone home to her parents to choose between him and me.

Now I'm so nervous. What can I do? How can I implore her to choose me? She's given me until February 1.

Here is a story about one of our old private railway lines (now closed down). The company once received a complaint from a man who had been bitten by a flea. By mistake he got his own letter back again, and discovered that a note had been scrawled on it: 'Send the idiot our duplicated Flea Letter No. 2.'

You mustn't take our advice in the same way when we say: 'We've got just the right answer for you. It's good and it's been tested.' The fact that it has been tested makes it all the better, doesn't it?

Well, then. You mustn't implore her to come back to you. It will only make the shackles seem heavier. On the contrary! With a swift movement you must sever those shackles which she perhaps finds oppressive.

In order to do this you must send the lady twenty-five dark red roses—no less. And the roses should be accompanied by a card, your visiting-card if you like, on which you must write:

Dear Eleanor (or whatever her name is)
Thank you for the time we have had together.
Thanks for—you!

John (or whatever your name is)

No more—and no less.

This piece of advice can also be used in the case of ladies who think they've made up their minds and gone. If there is the slightest chance of their feeling anything for the man they've abandoned, they'll come back—guaranteed!

It sounds like sorcery and strong medicine—and it is. But if every spark of tenderness in the lady has been extinguished, if the battle is really lost, without a shadow of doubt, then all the advice and sorcery in the world won't help.

May we moralize for a moment? This about her being so wonderful—we presume it's something you've known the whole time? And shown?

It's natural only to become fully aware of your feelings in your present position, but it's best for the relationship if you can show each other, in the course of everyday life, that you're fond of each other.

i. & s.h.

PS. May I tell you quite privately, dear writer, that I've seen this bit of advice work many times—every time. And may I add that I once asked my wife, in the days when we were just living together, how she would react if she left me and I sent her twenty-five roses with the above letter attached—and she answered:

'I'd come back!'

'Even if you knew it was a trick?'

'Oh yes! That doesn't make it any the less effective.'

s.h.

What Does a Girl do?

A long time ago you gave such a good answer to a man whose girl was about to leave him. But what does a girl do?

I agree with you entirely. I'd be touched to tears and fly straight back to him.

But can a girl send flowers? After all, in other situations it's always the man who has to take the first step—telephone or write —and then you just have to heave and sigh and long and wait for the telephone or the doorbell to ring, or for the postman to come. Am I too old-fashioned?

It certainly is an unsatisfactory state of affairs—that only the man is allowed to take the first step. Fortunately, bright girls have various ways of getting round things. They can ask a man if he could possibly give her a hand with this or that, make friends with his sister, etc. But it's still silly.

So much for the first step.

As far as the last step is concerned, if he wants to break off the relationship, then girls have opportunities too. They can send him, not twenty-five roses but, for example, a book called something like *When Bachelors Love*, or a box of cigars with a card saying: 'Here you are—just as a gesture of thanks for the time we've had together.'

It'll impress him.

i. & s.h.

Marriage

What is your opinion of marriage?

We've said this before, but it can't be said too often: marriage is not an institution that has been made to measure for human beings. It's something human beings have invented—a kind of emergency solution.

Some people think differently. There are people who believe that marriage, as an institution, enjoys the blessings of the powers that be. There are others who just feel that holy wedlock is a sort of cupboard in which two people can be locked up.

Both are dangerous attitudes, because they may result in people expecting too much of marriage—and doing too little about it themselves.

If, on the other hand, one believes that marriage isn't exactly an ideal institution, but is merely the best solution we happen to have at the moment to the problem of how two people should live together—then one also realizes that one shouldn't expect too much. Then one realizes that the cupboard may well start creaking at the joints now and then.

It is perhaps a sounder basis to get married on. The cupboard may last just a bit longer if one realizes it isn't the fault of human beings. It's the cupboard's fault if the space seems a bit restricted now and then.

It means, of course, that one shouldn't just assume that marriage is a marvellous state to have landed up in. It means one has to make an effort oneself—both the husband and the wife—to make it endurable.

And this may make it feel a little less like being locked up in a cupboard.

i. & s.h.

People are so Silly

I work in our town hall. I've got a desk next to the counter and have to talk to all sorts of people, but I can't stick it.

I've spoken to the head of our department about it, but he doesn't understand me. If only you knew how cross, grumpy and demanding people were these days!

How can I make my boss see that my job is an intolerable one, and that we must take turns at it?

We're only too happy to try to help you. But it will require a change of outlook on your part, no small amount of intelligence, self-knowledge and psychological sense. Do you think you can manage all that?

As the Danish author Scherfig has pointed out, people have an unfortunate tendency to criticize others with whom they have regular dealings. Telephonists seem to think that all subscribers are troublemakers or congenital idiots. Shop assistants are always imagining what a lot they'd get done if they weren't always interrupted by customers.

You'll have to take yourself by the proverbial scruff of the neck—which can be tricky, we know, but still. If you are honest and sweet and frank and helpful to the people who apply to you, you'll be rewarded by grateful smiles.

Now and then.   i. & s.h.

PS. Hans Scherfig, in his marvellous book, *The Neglected Spring*, tells of a group of ex-undergraduates who got together for a reunion twenty-five years later and exchanged experiences. The doctors spoke about their patients, and were able to relate the most incredible things about the ignorance and foolishness displayed by simple folk. The schoolmaster had a word or two to say about foolish schoolchildren. The lawyers described all the comical persons they'd met in the course of their practice. An army officer demonstrated that recruits weren't so very much better than patients. The judge had had the most extraordinary persons brought before him . . .

We could continue Scherfig's psychological observations. The grocer and the bank clerk could tell a tale or two about idiotic customers, the senior clerk in the Inland Revenue Department about foolish taxpayers, and the motor vehicle examiner about the sort of people who think they're fit to drive a car.

What's wrong? What is common to all these stories? In each case they concern the people our jobs bring us into daily contact with.

Well, the only explanation seems to be that there's something in the human make-up which makes us regard the people with whom we have to deal in our daily lives as our natural opponents. They are crazy, demanding, and out only to annoy us. In other words there's no real explanation, only a tendency in human nature which we must take due note of.

Is there nothing we can do about it?

We can make life unsatisfying for ourselves if we wallow in unhealthy attitudes. We've got to catch ourselves in the act, look nearer home and say: 'I'm the one to decide what these people are going to be like! I can make them sour, and I can make them happy. I can make them easy to get on with—or troublesome . . .

. . . and incidentally, they're the people I make my living from.'

i. & s.h.

Respect for the Experience

Both you and your wife are psychologists and have gone to university and have studied for many years.

Can you say, quite briefly, what you regard as the most important and useful thing you have learnt during your studies?

We can try.

If you ride a bicycle without a light and meet a policeman, you're frightened. If on the other hand you are attacked by a gang of rowdies, and the same policeman comes to your assistance, you're delighted. Physically speaking, the policeman is the same in both cases. But you experience him differently.

If a patient complains to his doctor and says 'Doctor, I'm feeling so dreadful!' and the doctor examines him and says 'Nonsense, there's nothing wrong with you!'—the patient is the one who's in the right. It's quite correct that the doctor was unable to find anything physically wrong with the patient, but the patient really *felt* dreadful—this was how he experienced it —and this we must respect.

When you study psychology it is impressed upon you very strongly that you must differentiate very clearly between what can be measured in physical terms and what is actually experienced. This is perhaps the most important thing you learn as a budding psychologist: respect for the experience.

This respect for the fact that others can experience the same thing in a different way is something we all have need of every day. Not only in marriage, where we have to face the fact that our partner may see certain things differently ... against a different background.

The young man whose parents always bathed naked together with their children simply cannot understand why his young wife, who comes from a home where a much more prudish outlook prevailed, finds it very difficult to take off all her clothes.

Just to take an example.

i. & s.h.

Easy Way to Make a Living

My wife is pregnant and now five months gone. We're so excited. We already have a son and would so badly like to have a daughter.

Is it possible to find out beforehand?

As far as we remember, it is possible to have the sex of a child determined before birth ... But it's so risky that it is very seldom done unless there are very weighty reasons for it.

Did you know, by the way, that swindlers exist who make easy livings for themselves out of this very question?

We'll tell you how. The swindler buys a great big ledger and puts an advertisement in the paper:

WE CAN PROPHESY THE SEX OF YOUR CHILD!
ARE YOU PREGNANT? SEND 2 SHILLINGS!

And then, when John Smith asks, the answer comes right back: 'You will have a daughter!' But in the big black ledger the swindler writes: 'John Smith will have *a son.*'

Now the swindle is waterproof. Either John Smith has a daughter and is perfectly satisfied with the answer he got—or else he has a son and can't be bothered to kick up a fuss. In a very few instances, John Smith will go along to the swindler and say: 'What the hell's the idea? You promised me a daughter, and all I got was a son!' The swindler looks up John Smith in the big black ledger and says: 'It seems there's been an unfortunate error, sir. Look! You can see for yourself. Here it says quite clearly: "Mr John Smith informed 15th June that he would have a son".'

We won't swindle. We'll use a psychological trick and say: We're quite sure you'll have a daughter!

If you have a daughter you'll be impressed by us. If you have a son, you'll say: 'Heavens, they're nice people, they couldn't help it—they did their best.'

i. & s.h.

Postscript

We repeat that nobody has paid us for mentioning their names or their products in this book—not in cash, in kind, or in any other way.

Being mentioned is not in itself a recommendation on our part. All we have tried to do, in the interests of consumers, is to indicate a few possibilities.

The market in this field is so variable, and developing so fast, that a certain amount of the information we have given may well be out-of-date before the book is published. We have by no means managed to include everything.

i. & s.h.

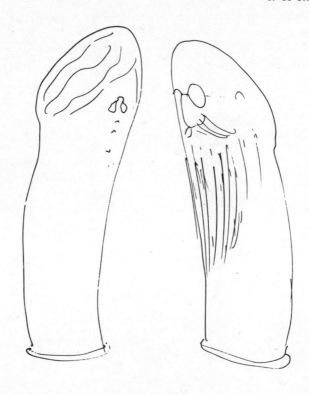

Index